DATE DUE

Demco, Inc. 38-293

Discovering Programs for Talent Development

To Chris, Carlyn, and Janna
Everything

Discovering Programs for Talent Development

Beverly N. Parke

CORWIN PRESS, INC.
A Sage Publications Company
Thousand Oaks, California

For information:

Corwin Press, Inc.
A Sage Publications Company
2455 Teller Road
Thousand Oaks, California 91320
www.corwinpress.com

Sage Publications Ltd.
6 Bonhill Street
London EC2A 4PU
United Kingdom

Sage Publications India Pvt. Ltd.
M-32 Market
Greater Kailash I
New Delhi 110 048 India

Printed in the United States of America

Library of Congress Cataloging-in-Publication Data

Parke, Beverly N.
Discovering programs for talent development / Beverly N. Parke.
        p. cm.
Includes bibliographical references and index.
ISBN 0-7619-4612-8 (c) -- ISBN 0-7619-4613-6 (p)
    1. Gifted children—Education—United States. I. Title.
LC3993.9 .P36 2003
371.95--dc211

                                            2002010380

This book is printed on acid-free paper.

03 04 05 06 07 7 6 5 4 3 2 1

Acquisitions Editor:	Kylee Liegl
Production Editor:	Olivia Weber
Typesetter/Designer:	C&M Digitals (P) Ltd
Indexer:	Julie Grayson
Cover Designer:	Tracy E. Miller
Production Artist:	Janet Foulger

Contents

Preface

Advocates for gifted and talented students have been working for decades in an attempt to bring full service to this population. Under a full-service model, students of high ability are in educational programs that are challenging and coordinate with their unique needs. Such a situation is rare despite the efforts of professionals throughout the educational spectrum. This situation is due to many factors, all of which are important and need to be addressed. In the meantime, thousands of students are in educational environments that do not correspond to their advanced abilities.

In a prior book, *Gifted Students in Regular Classrooms* (Parke, 1989), I addressed the need for gifted and talented students, placed in regular classroom structures, to receive appropriate programming options. At first this concept met with a great deal of criticism from professional colleagues, as they were concerned that this point of view could jeopardize efforts to build specialized classes outside the regular classroom for these students. "Why would you write a book about this topic if it means people use it as an excuse to cut the few programs that are already in place?" My rationale was simple. For the most part, gifted and talented students spend the vast majority of their time *in* general-education classrooms. It is essential that the instruction they receive, wherever that may be, coordinate with the learning needs they possess. Teachers need to be trained to organize their classrooms to deal with the multiple abilities their students display. I had hoped that my book would be just a small part of that effort. From the response the book received after publication, I believe I met that goal.

Unfortunately, the students' situation has not changed a great deal. Gifted and talented students are still receiving the bulk of their instruction through the general-education structure (Westberg, Archambault, Dobyns, & Slavin, 1992). Advocates continue to lobby policymakers from local school boards, intermediate districts, state boards of education, and Washington, D.C., for additional funds and program offerings. Surprisingly, the concern for potential student underachievement has not been seriously addressed at the local level despite the current school reform initiatives. The change that has been called for has yet to emerge.

What has changed is the voice from within the gifted-child education field. Openly, people are discussing the value of modifying the name under which programs are organized. The question is asked, "Can we be more successful in developing a full-service model for these students if we find a new label for their needs?" The label in dispute is *gifted*. It connotes students who have an advantage that has not been afforded to all. The label comes under attack because it sounds as if the students to whom it is attached are "special" in some way rather than "different" in their learning needs. In a country where we value the rags-to-riches stories and applaud those who have lived the American dream, it is difficult to sell the idea that there are students who are at risk due to their capability. The question continues to be asked, "Why funnel resources to a population that is already ahead of the game?"

The question deserves an answer rather than indignation. Perhaps a new label would make serious discussions more likely to result in change. Maybe the research being federally funded at the National Research Center on the Gifted and Talented, University of Connecticut, Storrs, will establish *difference* and *need* in a way that will be understood and addressed by those who control program design and funding. Possibly, the emergence of the multiple-intelligence models (Gardner, 1983; Sternberg, 1986; Wagner, 2000) will be the basis for a fresh restructuring of educational instruction that will be matched to the multiple talents of students.

Perhaps . . . maybe . . . perchance . . . conceivably . . . possibly . . . These words provide little comfort for the students, parents, and teachers who are currently part of our educational systems. They need some degree of relief now. Under the circumstances of limited funds and expanding expectations, what can reasonably be done? There are answers, and that is the topic of this book.

It is my hope that this book will give these constituencies a new perspective on the topic of program development for students with exceptional ability. I take a talent development perspective and apply it to a program mosaic model. My contention is that there are many programs, currently on the books and readily accepted, through which talented students can find challenge and growth of their abilities. These are programs that are not under the aegis of gifted-child education but can be adopted to create a more appropriate educational experience for this population.

I do wish to offer one caution to the reader. The philosophy behind and content of *Discovering Programs for Talent Development* should not be used as a platform for dismantling programs currently offered for talented students. Programmatic suggestions that appear here should be supplemental to the rigorous programs currently offered. The needs of these students are so vast, and the program development needed so daunting, that making the best use of all resources available is essential. It is to this end that I offer this book.

Finally, I would like to relate a story that was told to me through a holiday card this season (thanks, Cindy). The Masai tribe of Africa has a greeting that they use to acknowledge those they meet. The greeting is, "How are the children?" This is not reserved for those who have children. Rather, it is a way to recognize that the children are the focus of the tribe. I end with the same question, *"How are the children?"*

ACKNOWLEDGMENTS ◾

Unbelievably, the idea for this book was formulated during my annual review interview at Indiana University Purdue University Ft. Wayne. This is certainly testament to the notion that you never know when your thinking will be challenged and a change will occur in the way you perceive the world and the elements within it. Dr. David McCants was the person on the other side of the table that day, and to him I owe a debt of gratitude for engaging the discussion that led to this book. I also would like to take this opportunity to acknowledge my colleagues and students who have contributed the context and inspiration for this work. To the staff at Corwin, Robb Clouse and Kylee Liegl in particular, thank you for encouraging my ideas and working to bring them to publication. I would also like to acknowledge Hawley Roddick, who offered her amazing editorial expertise to this project.

My colleagues at Corwin and I gratefully acknowledge the contributions of the following reviewers:

Mary K. Tallent-Runnels, PhD
   Texas Tech University
   Lubbock, TX

Tracy L. Cross, PhD
   Ball State University
   Muncie, IN

Felicia A. Dixon, PhD
   Ball State University
   Muncie, IN

Cynthia Martone, EdD
   Holmes Road Elementary School
   Rochester, NY

About the Author

Beverly N. Parke, PhD, is a member of the School of Education faculty at Indiana University Purdue University Ft. Wayne where she teaches courses in Special Education. Her primary research and writing emphasis is on program options for exceptional children.

She is the author of two books, *Discovering Programs for Talent Development* (Corwin, 2002) and *Gifted Students in Regular Classrooms* (1989) as well as over 30 other publications and a software package. In addition, she has served as president of The Association for Gifted and editor of *Journal for the Education of the Gifted.* She is the recipient of the *Certificate of Merit* (1996), given for exemplary service to gifted-child education from The Association for Gifted. She has delivered keynote speeches on gifted-child education throughout the United States and Canada.

At this time, she is engaged in two research projects. One involves the outcomes of dual-enrollment programs for high school students attending universities. The other looks at the effects of early-childhood intervention programs on children at risk for success in kindergarten.

She is married to her husband of 23 years, Christopher, and is the mother of two daughters, Carlyn and Janna.

1

Uncovering Hidden Programs

"Thank you for attending your parent-teacher conference, Mrs. Richardson. I am anxious to talk to you about the great opportunities in store for Sophie next year. She has been recommended and accepted for PACE, the gifted and talented program here at Greenwood Middle School. It meets every Thursday afternoon for 2 hours. We're thrilled that she will have the chance to work with students of similar abilities and explore her interest in mathematics."

"That certainly is good news," responded Mrs. Richardson. "You know, Mr. Spence, that we have long thought Sophie needed some extra work beyond what she is getting in the regular classroom. I'm glad she'll finally have the opportunity to get that through PACE. I have only one concern. Sophie is a very intelligent and talented child. Her abilities are not only in the area of mathematics. What will be available to her in the sciences and arts? You know she excels in those areas, too."

Countless parents and teachers have engaged in similar conversations as they have struggled to extend appropriate educational opportunities to the gifted and talented students in their charge. The answer given to Mrs. Richardson's query is telling:

"Mrs. Richardson, we are well aware of your daughter's capabilities in the areas of science and the arts. At this time, our program for gifted and talented students focuses only on the area of mathematics. We are fortunate to have that! There are indications that if the math program continues to be such a success and is supported by the parents, community, and educational staff, we may be able to extend it to other content areas in the future. For now, though, math is it. Hopefully, Sophie's other teachers will provide special assignments and activities for her in the classroom."

The result of this type of meeting is bittersweet. Parents and educators alike are thrilled—and relieved—that the student will be included in a program that is designed to meet the needs of a high-ability person. On the other hand, both are aware that there are other needs left unmet. Many express the sentiment that at least *something* is being done. They often report that attending a program like PACE, that is suited to the unique needs of the child, is what keeps that child coming to school. As for Mrs. Richardson, she is encouraged that Sophie may finally be involved in mathematics suited to her performance level but laments the fact that her talents in science and art may still go unchallenged and underdeveloped.

But, is that truly the case? Has Mr. Spence accurately portrayed the educational program available to Sophie and other students at Greenwood Middle School? Before answering that question, it is essential to explore the possibility that there may be hidden programs at Greenwood that are effectively serving gifted and talented students. Such programs may not have the gifted and talented designation. The absence of that title, however, should not be used as a reason to discount potential growth opportunities embedded within such programs. Schools sponsor many activities that extend students' talents in significant ways even though they do not come under the auspices of a gifted-child education program. These hidden programs may offer substantial educational experiences for high-ability students and are potentially an integral part of a full service paradigm.

■ CHALLENGING CONVENTIONAL WISDOM

Traditionally, schools have had difficulty gaining support for establishing programs for their gifted and talented students. The reasons for the hesitancy are numerous (Sapon-Shevin, 1994). They extend from arguments within and outside the educational structure but usually center on matters of finances, philosophy, transportation, and scheduling. Too often, trivial matters intervene and opportunities are lost.

One outcome from this decades-long struggle is that many districts are satisfied to have any program on the books. After years of debate, they settle on one programming option and have little energy or desire to push for extending programs into new content areas. For the most part, school districts have a single program for the gifted at each level—usually a resource room or honors program. It will most likely comprise students from one grade level who show exceptional talent. Chances are the teacher is one of the best in the district, and the students eagerly devour their activities. The ideas and dialogue that take place, even with the youngest of participants, inspire students and teachers alike.

While a program may be all one could ask for and more, parents and educators are often left wondering if enough is being done. "What is happening for these students the rest of the day? Are they truly being challenged? What capabilities are going underdeveloped in this unitary approach to educating students?" These are haunting questions that are mostly answered by unsatisfactory responses. Who knows what possibilities are lost when youths are rarely challenged?

The educational community is well aware of the inadequacy of the present system. It is also highly defensive of the general education curriculum—and rightfully so. With the current reform movements (Gallagher & Coleman, 1995; Gallagher & Sapon-Shevin, 1997) and emphasis on best practice (Fogarty, 1995; Zemelman, Daniels, & Hyde, 1993), a great deal of time and effort is being spent to improve the educational system from top to bottom. Parents are not alone in wanting what is best for their children. Educators select teaching as their profession because they hold a strong commitment to the students that they work with daily.

Surprisingly, they have been about the business of talent development in ways in which even they are often not aware. In fact, they have been developing programs well suited to the gifted and talented for years, but have not affixed a gifted and talented designation to what the programs do. It is these programs that often remain hidden when discussing the offerings available to high-ability students. Typical offerings such as student council, debate, student newspaper, and science fair are all examples of frequently found programs that serve the needs of gifted and talented students in significant ways. They are not programs established solely for the gifted and talented. However, high-ability students profit from participation in such programs as they provide a structure through which they can develop skills and knowledge in ways that are appropriate to their unique learning needs. These are not programs exclusively for the gifted and talented, but they are programs that involve these students with effective results.

The Association for Gifted (1989) recognized this fact when it issued the seminal publication *Standards for Programs Involving the Gifted and Talented*. It is the innovative premise of this guide that when evaluating program efficacy, it is essential that all programs in which these students are engaged be held accountable for meeting their educational needs. It is also an underlying philosophical position that programs do not need to be designated as gifted and talented in order to be a significant contributing force to the education of these students. This leaves a broad spectrum of program possibilities when considering the question, "What constitutes appropriate programming for gifted and talented students?" In essence, many programs are in play. When deciding if a program option matches the learning needs of an individual student, the directing question is not, "Is this a gifted and talented program?" Rather, the question is, "Does this program meet the learning needs of this gifted and talented student?"

This change in conventional wisdom is essential to see the full scope of programming opportunities available to these students. Such change does come with a crucial caution, however. Not all programs are appropriate for high-ability students. If that were the case, the struggle to assemble challenging programs for these students would evaporate. In Sophie's case, while only the PACE program was available through the sponsorship of the gifted child education department, there most assuredly were other activities and programs that corresponded to her abilities, interests, and needs in the sciences and arts. When responding to Mrs. Richardson's query about the programming options available to Sophie, Mr. Spence could have accurately highlighted Sophie's participation in Arts United, Monarch Watch, and her lab assistant position. The opportunities available to Sophie went beyond the boundaries of PACE and could be represented as potential optional activities when discussing a full-service program that corresponded to her profile of ability (see Chapter 3 for more on profiles).

An abundance of programs from which gifted and talented students can benefit is hidden in every school district. One need only peruse the yearbook, student newspaper, community education class offerings, after-school program brochures, or home newsletter to find numerous examples. However, the search should not stop there. To fully expose hidden programs, community offerings should also be explored. Internships, 4-H clubs, volunteering, and Junior Achievement are among the community-based programs from which high-ability students can profit. Even a family trip and dress-up box hold a wealth of potential for expanding the capabilities of young people. The search for opportunities to develop talent should not be narrow and should not be confined to school-sponsored programs. In order to develop well-rounded opportunities for personal growth, all avenues should be considered. With the guidance of such people as parents, educators, mentors, counselors, and other students, the gifted and talented can be part of challenging programming efforts that expand their abilities and perception of the world.

■ WHY PROGRAMS REMAIN HIDDEN

Only one explanation lies at the root of why many programs, that could appropriately serve gifted and talented students, remain hidden. There is a misconception that specialized programs for these students are the only settings in which their needs are well served. This simply is not the case. In fact, varied experiences far better serve this population than one set track. Gifted and talented students, like all students, have a variety of abilities and interests. Rarely will one program focus on all of these areas. Therefore multiple options are necessary. Unfortunately, the program for gifted and talented students is unlikely to be in a position to sponsor them all, as resources are rarely sufficient.

This is not to say that programs specifically designed for the gifted and talented are not a vital component of a full-service approach to programming for these students. They absolutely are! The need for rigor in academic programs is essential and must be the linchpin of any effort toward talent development. There is no replacement for challenging content in academic programs. The premise of this discussion is that it may well be necessary to augment the standard program for these students with additional options in order to fully meet the learning needs of the gifted and talented. Options are there for the discovery.

The PACE program is an excellent alternative for Sophie and essential to her growth and development in mathematics. However, other options are needed to deal with her precocity in science and arts. As the district has yet to develop programs for gifted and talented middle schoolers in these content areas, it is to the hidden programs that Mrs. Richardson and Mr. Spence must look. Chances are, they will find additional options for Sophie that will enhance her talent development. The concern that nothing is being done beyond PACE can rapidly vanish as a more complete combination of responsive programming is constructed.

BUILDING PROGRAM ■
MOSAICS FOR FULL SERVICE

The goal of education is to expand students' abilities—not to establish programs. It does little good to offer programming options geared to the gifted if none meet the needs of a particular child. Advocates for gifted and talented students are well advised to promote the expansion of multiple programming options throughout the curriculum (Shore, Cornell, Robinson, & Ward, 1991) so matches to individual talents are more available. Some options may only target the needs of highly gifted students, while others may focus on a broader population. It is through the construction of comprehensive individual programs that learning needs are met.

It is useful to compare the process of building programming options to that of assembling a mosaic (Parke, 1989). An artistic vision inspires a mosaic built from many shards of glass or clay. Artists piece together individual shards of varying colors, intensities, and shapes to represent their ideas—an expression of their vision. Individual pieces flow together to create one mosaic, each piece serving its own function for the whole. When one piece is chipped or missing, the entire mosaic is less satisfying. It requires the whole of the parts to bring forth the complex totality of the artistic experience.

So it is in assembling programs for gifted and talented students. One option or piece will not satisfy the whole. Individual pieces must be carefully meshed to jointly create fully responsive programs for the students. Options must be mixed and matched to the students' profile of ability. It is impossible to accomplish this task using only one programmatic component. Variety is essential in order to correspond with the individuality students bring to the process. Programming options, assembled into a comprehensive program mosaic, establish the best chance students have to attain the ultimate goal that is full service. Missing pieces result in missed opportunities and promise unfulfilled.

Expanding the vision of what might be may buttress the fragile assemblage of programming for the gifted and talented. It requires motivation and insight to break the boundaries of traditional thinking and move to the basics of matching learning need to program options. The more unusual the learning need—the more creative the option needed to address that need. With the remarkable talents and interests displayed by high-ability students, program planners and parents are often left with a challenging task. Finding appropriate options can be difficult and requires patience, innovation, and a willingness to question conventional practice.

The rewards for the students are great. When a child's picture graces the cover of the annual report of a local business, a student-submitted editorial appears in the local newspaper, or the first annual, districtwide arts festival is the brainchild of program students, it is clear that the outcome was worth the effort. This type of opportunity makes a true impact on the lives and talents of the students. It is no fluke that these are the experiences students later remember from their school days. For it is through intimate expression that personal growth occurs. Bringing talent to bear upon challenging tasks and emerging with distinctive outcomes moves students forward in their quest for meaning.

■ CONCLUSION

Educators and parents of talented students face an ongoing challenge of identifying programming options that correspond to the varied abilities of youths. The range of abilities seen in this group requires creative program development if full service is to be an actuality. Assembling program mosaics is one way to attain this goal. Mosaics become possible when shards are assembled and arranged. Full service can be a reality when a mosaic of programming options is created. From this array, the mixing and matching of program options to personal profiles of ability can commence. As all students bring a unique pattern of talents and interests to their educational experience, a corresponding program mosaic can be constructed to further illuminate these patterns and extend them to new expressions of ability.

■ POINTS TO PONDER

- Full service is possible for gifted and talented students.
- One program option for students of varied talents is not sufficient.
- Multiple programming options are needed.
- Individual profiles of ability are necessary and are to be matched to programming options to create full service for talented students.
- Programming options that serve talented students may well be hidden when they do not carry a label (e.g., honors, gifted) indicating a program that is targeting high-ability students.
- Program planners must be creative and far-reaching in their assembly of programming options for this population.

2

Revealing Talent

Needless to say, Mr. Spence was concerned about his conversation with Mrs. Richardson regarding her daughter Sophie (see Chapter 1). Her comments troubled him for days:

> I know we are a first-rate school in academics, sports, and the arts. But, are there opportunities through which students of Sophie's caliber can work beyond what is typically taught through the general-education curriculum? There must be other students in Sophie's situation. I wonder which forms of talent our schools are focusing on? Which are neglected? If we want to be a first-rate school, I had better investigate this further.

What Mr. Spence discovered immediately altered his perspectives on ability and set him on a new path. His insights follow.

IDEAS ABOUT TALENT ■

Few educators have applied for a position in which they would work with gifted and talented students without first being asked the question, "What is the difference between giftedness and talent?" Interviewees squirm anticipating the question as it is a difficult one to answer. Prepared candidates may cite one of the following responses. "Giftedness is a cognitive process and talent is a physical process." "Giftedness is an extreme form of talent." Or, "Talent encompasses giftedness." The question has never been answered with a distinction that all will accept.

Ambivalence toward these terms has been seen as a primary impediment in the quest toward full service for these students. Gagne (1995) writes, "Because these two terms play such a central role, one would think that much care was taken to define them precisely so that all members of the field would share a common vision of their specific meaning" (p. 103). Obviously, this has not been the case. This controversy can leave the impression that the field is weak and borders on irrelevant. After all, if those who know the most about exceptional ability cannot agree on terms and definitions, how can they expect other educators to understand the parameters of this field, much less support its programs?

Many program planners feel the label *gifted* is an actual ally for those who seek to sabotage attempts for differentiating curriculum. Gallagher (1991) writes,

> *Gifted*, as a term, carries the surplus meaning to many persons in our society of unjustified and unearned privilege. It represents to many a similar concept of "inherited wealth." It appears to invoke images of a ruling elite of the type we fought in the American Revolution. The extension of such a situation through public education seems to some as not merely wrong, but morally offensive. (p. 355)

The following comments are familiar to those advocating specialized programs for the gifted.

- Schools should be teaching the basics. This idea that schools should be encouraging "talent" is a waste of time.
- I haven't had a "gifted" student in all my years of teaching. No Einsteins have been in this room.
- These programs are elitist, as they include only the best of the best.
- If you want to talk about gifted, let's talk about the students who are doing so poorly they could use a gift of additional resources.
- All students are gifted in one way or another.
- If they are so good, why do they need special programs? They can make it on their own.
- Our programs are strong. We don't need to provide specialized programs. We are meeting the needs of our students within our general-education offerings.

These points of view have led those involved in gifted-child education to consider the possibility of simply replacing the term *gifted* as a way to break down the endless semantic roadblocks. Why fight the battle over terminology when the real goal is to provide challenging programs for the students? Terms such as *high ability, high achieving, academically talented, adept, exceptional,* and *above average* have been used in an attempt to find more broadly agreeable labels. Some school districts have solved the problem by simply using acronyms to distinguish services for these students from the norm. Thus you will hear students being referred to as eagles, or members of the TAG, LEAP, or GATE programs at their schools.

A serious academic debate about this dilemma has begun in earnest. How these terms relate to one another has been the source of a great deal of writing over the past decade (Feldhusen, 1994; Renzulli, 1994b; VanTassel-Baska, 1998). Perhaps the most visible publication has been a seminal document issued through the U.S. Department of Education (USDE) (1993). It features the term *talent* in a different context from in the past, as it offers the first major change in the official definition of giftedness in 20 years. It states that gifted learners are

> Children and youth with outstanding talent who perform or show the potential for performing at remarkably high levels of accomplishment when compared to others of their age, experience, or environment. These children and youth exhibit high performance capability in intellectual, creative, and/or artistic areas, possess an unusual leadership capacity, or excel in specific academic fields. They require services or activities not ordinarily provided by the schools. Outstanding talents are present in children and youth from all cultural groups, across all economic strata, and in all areas of human endeavor. (p. 26)

While there is no groundswell of opinion to drop the term *gifted* from the nomenclature of the field, its predominance in research and application has become more balanced with the emergence of talent as a serious partner in identification and program development. This is due to a number of factors in addition to the issuance of the USDE (1993) document. The work of many of the most eminent scholars in the field (e.g., Feldhusen, 1998; Gagne, 1995; Gallagher, 1991; Gardner, 1997; Renzulli, 1998; Sternberg, 1990; Treffinger, 1998; VanTassel-Baska, 1998) prominently feature the concept of talent as an important component of models for students with high ability. The nationwide emphasis on school improvement (Gallagher & Coleman, 1995) has also played a role, as has the wide-scale application of Gardner's model of multiple intelligences (MI) (Gardner, 1983).

During this time, numerous viewpoints have been presented as the proponents of a more visible role for talent development have begun to state their case in earnest. Feldhusen (1995), one of the leading advocates of a talent development model, asserts, "The field that we called gifted education . . . is now becoming the field of talent development" (p. 92). His viewpoint is supported by Gagne (1995) who adds, "The development of talents, whether in academic subjects or in other fields of human activity should in my view be the primary goal of our field." Treffinger (1995) continues, stating the

> Trend towards a talent development approach represents a deep or fundamental new orientation concerning the nature, scope, and practice of our field, and thus involves challenges for growth and change in areas that are deeply embedded in the history and traditions of gifted education. (p. 94)

These calls for change have been buttressed with proposed definitions of talent that can be used as a foundation for program development.

DEFINITIONS OF TALENT ■

Gagne (1995) provides definitions of giftedness and talent that offer a distinction between the terms. He defines each as follows: Gifted refers to

> The possession and use of untrained and spontaneously expressed natural abilities (called aptitudes or gifts) in at least one ability domain, to a degree that places the child or adult at least among the top 15% of his or her age peers. (p. 106)

He suggests using measures of aptitude or natural ability to make the determination. Talent is defined as

> The superior mastery of systematically developed abilities (or skills) and knowledge in at least one field of human activity, to a degree that places a child's or adult's achievement within at least the upper 15% of his or her age peers who are active in that field or fields. (p. 106)

Measures of developed skills are suggested as tools for identification of talent. He summarizes his point of view by stating,

> Giftedness refers to measures of potential, of untrained natural abilities, while the term "talent" is reserved specifically for indices of achievement, of the performance attained as the result of a systematic program of training and practice. Only if the target population has been selected using both types of measures, aptitude as well as achievement, does logic demand that both labels be applied. (p. 106)

Under this paradigm, then, a person would be talented through achievement in a particular area as opposed to having unusually high natural ability (which may or not be developed) and, thus, being categorized more commonly by the term gifted.

Treffinger (1998) offers an alternate definition of talent. He proposes that talent be defined as "the potential for significant creative contributions or productivity in any domain of inquiry, expression, or action over an extended period of time" (p. 753). It is his belief that the field of gifted-child education should adopt this broader definition of talent and move beyond the classic belief that there is a measurable set of cognitive abilities that are minimally influenced by the environment. Rather, he suggests that the field embrace a broader array of abilities or talents.

Regardless of the preferred definition, those proposing a shift to a more talent-based model agree that the "goal is to find an appropriate educational response" (Treffinger, 1998, p. 754) for these students. In a field that has spent decades trying to establish who the truly gifted are, this move toward full-programmatic service is a welcome departure.

■ TALENTS LIGHT THE WAY

Under a talent model, thinking of program options in terms of both giftedness and talent finds previously hidden programs becoming more apparent. Schools sponsor numerous programs drawing on a wide variety of student talent but are often unaware that these options may effectively serve talented students as part of a full-service model. Mr. Spence found that he could easily draw from a wide program base when constructing an appropriate program for Sophie. He now understood that identifying experiences that matched Sophie's needs was the primary goal, not finding classes marked gifted and talented. For program appropriateness cannot be determined by program title.

As Mr. Spence was reflecting on this new insight, he found himself laughing out loud as he reminisced about a past student named Drew. Mrs. Lindsey, Drew's first grade teacher, had recounted the following story to Mr. Spence:

> It was just about time to clean up from science and go to the cafeteria for lunch. As usual, I asked the students if anyone needed a lunch charge slip. Drew raised his hand. I had a hard time keeping a straight face as he informed me of his problem. "I seem to have a cash-flow problem. May I have a charge slip?" Can you believe a 6-year-old would say this, much less in correct context? I called his mom to share the story and found her to be less than surprised. Evidently, she had just gotten off the phone with Drew's bus driver, who was seeking her help. It seems the other students were paying Drew for the opportunity to sit next to him on the bus. He obviously is an emerging entrepreneur. I just know that we need to be channeling Drew toward positive outlets for his articulate and creative mind. Otherwise, I am afraid we will be having less comical and more disruptive behaviors in the future.

Recalling Drew's story reinforced Mr. Spence's determination to explore Greenwood's curricular options including, but not limited to, PACE (see Chapter 1). Addressing the obvious variance in student abilities no longer seemed like an unwieldy task. A talent-based approach would serve their needs well, and the educational community and its stakeholders were likely to embrace it. It became his commitment to ensure that all Greenwood students were enrolled in program opportunities matching their profile of ability (more about POAs later in the chapter).

MULTIPLE INTELLIGENCES MODEL   ■

To address the same issues targeted by Mr. Spence, many schools are being redesigned (Bellanca, 1998) based on the work of Gardner (1983, 1997). For the past two decades, he has been developing an alternative concept of intelligence. Not content with the historical definition of intelligence that postulates a single factor accounting for ability (Spearman, 1927), Gardner has brought forth his own research-based model that describes a constellation of intelligences. The MI model breaks intelligence into eight equally essential parts. These are spatial, logical and mathematical, linguistic, musical, bodily kinesthetic, interpersonal, intrapersonal, and environmental intelligence. Gardner (1999) believes that the intelligences found in each individual are in any combination of strength and weakness. It is from this variance that individual differences emerge. Sophie finds her strength through the spatial and logical-mathematical segments while still showing

Table 2.1
Sample Mosaic
Options

MI Intelligence Category	Mosaic Component	Activity for Home
Linguistic	Foreign Languages	Puppet Show
Bodily Kinesthetic	Advanced Dance	Backyard Gymnastics
Musical	Show Choir	Flute Lessons
Spatial	Architecture for Children	Sandbox Castles
Interpersonal	Peer Mediation	Dinner Table Discussions
Logical/Mathematical	Philosophy for Kids	Building Birdhouses
Environmental	Pond Investigations	Nature Walks
SOURCE: H. Gardner (1983).		

evidence of substantial intelligence in many of the other six segments. They are just not as pronounced. Drew is advanced in the linguistic and interpersonal areas. Lesley, a talented golfer at Greenwood Middle School, finds strength through the intelligences that govern spatial and bodily kinesthetic abilities. An even higher level of accomplishment may be found when intelligences are teamed, resulting in exceptional achievement.

When Mr. Spence discovered the MI model, it was a catalytic moment. He now could see how his nephew, a divinity student, might express intelligence in all areas but most fully in interpersonal and intrapersonal skills. Musical intelligence could combine with other intelligences to explain some of the precocity displayed by Ashlyn, the first-chair violinist in the youth orchestra. As there is no hierarchy within the MI model, no one intelligence is deemed superior to others. Elegantly, the issue of elitism, ever a primary concern when using the term gifted, disappears. Together, intelligences are jumbled within each person resulting in *proclivities*—not just a single intellectual ability.

Using MI as a theoretical base, educators have found a roadmap to full-service. They can easily take each intelligence, match it to curricular and extracurricular activities, and determine where strengths and weaknesses occur in an overall school program (see Table 2.1). Gaps can become the focus upon which program development and school redesign is directed. With so many variations possible, schools emerge with distinct personalities reflecting their student bodies. Their programmatic makeup can change from year to year. The trick for program designers is to create a mosaic of programmatic experiences (Parke, 1989) that is responsive to the talents and abilities of each student presently enrolled. This is and will be an ongoing task for those doing curricular design as Gardner continues to expand his model.

Parents of talented students are also well-advised by the MI model. Becoming aware of the intelligences targeted by Gardner allows parents to view the family and their activities more broadly. For example, a typical conundrum faced by parents has to do with the ever-difficult decision of whether or not to acquiesce to a child's desire to stop piano lessons at an age they deem too early. The debate often comes down to an argument spurred by concern centered on the danger that a decision to stop will, in some way, harm the child in the long term. Potential harm is usually predicted in the areas of perseverance or skill. When the concern is put into the context of MI, one sees musical talent as part of the larger intellectual whole in which children may or may not excel to a high level. Should the parents allow a child to stop piano lessons? The answer is rarely a simple yes or no. If the lessons are considered in tandem with the other areas of intelligence explicit in MI, parents can evaluate the total balance of their children's activities. Does the child want to try other areas of music? Has the playing of the piano developed to the point that a pedestrian level of skill is present? Is the child showing interest and skill development in other areas?

What is the goal? How is it served by continuing the lessons? If the child intends to be a pianist accompanying an orchestra, prematurely discontinuing lessons is problematic. On the other hand, if the child is already adequately skilled in other musical endeavors (e.g., choir, trombone, or marching band), discontinuing piano instruction may free up time to explore other MI areas or delve more fully into an alternative area of musical interest. The decision is rarely clear-cut, but when taken within the context of the MI model, how this decision balances out may be seen more holistically.

From either point of view, school-based or home-based, the MI model is useful in developing a point of reference for activities. Are there opportunities within the school environment to develop and extend ability in each area of the MI model? Are there opportunities within the family's activities that provide the child with well-rounded developmental opportunities? Is there a complimentary convergence of activity? If so, it is likely that there is opportunity for a child's talent development. If there are gaps, the child may be at risk when potential is compared to achievement. Using MI as a basis for judgment, either the school, home, or a combination of both can extend current practices to more fully assist the student in developing abilities.

Gardner is not the only cognitive psychologist to tackle the issues inherent in the great debate as to how intelligence is configured. Significant work by Sternberg (1986) has also explored the nature of intelligence. His model comprises three components and is also useful when evaluating a student's activities and the potential for a high level of intellectual development.

DEFINING CHARACTERISTICS OF TALENTED STUDENTS ■

The only way differentiated programming can be viable for students is if it is built on individual differences and resulting need. Elitism is a frequent charge used to attack programs designed to assist students of high ability. This charge primarily stems from student identification systems that favor students with general abilities rather than specific aptitudes. When few programs exist for the highly talented student, there is a temptation to place all high-ability students in the programs that do exist, appropriate or not. The convoluted rationale, "Well, something is better than nothing," can provide an excuse to leave students underserved. It also gives persons claiming elitism a viable example to point out.

If a student has outstanding ability in mathematics but not in literature, it does not make sense to place that child in a high ability-class discussing creative writing, even if it is the only class offered for high-ability students. Such placement decisions not only compromise the growth of the student but they also weaken the class and its desired outcomes.

Classes designed specifically for students with unusually advanced talent are appropriate and nonelitist only when they are composed of the students who can successfully complete rigorous requirements. Students of lesser ability, if enrolled in the class, should be unable to attain the program goals at an adequate level, as course requirements should exceed their achievement and ability levels. Only those students appropriately matched to a class should have the capacity to succeed. If others are enrolled, for whatever reason, the class is likely to be made easier so all students can succeed, thus changing the intensity and purpose of the class. Or else it is clearly elitist in its inclusion of some and exclusion of others for reasons other than a precise match between students' needs and course goals.

In order to provide challenging programs for talented students, it is essential that the characteristics that distinguish these students from their age or class peers be identified. This distinction is what must direct program planning and leads to successfully developing substantial programming options (Cox, Daniel, & Boston, 1985) suited to the students' learning needs. When students who are eligible for the program possess capabilities needed for program success, such programs are also ethically viable.

Pace, Depth, and Interest

Students who learn at a pace that substantially surpasses their peers are among those most easily and typically identified as gifted. Programs based on accelerated content or subject matter are also appropriate matches for the highly talented. Advanced placement (VanTassel-Baska, 2001), honors classes, grade skipping, Curriculum Compacting (Renzulli, Smith, & Reis, 1982), and computer-assisted instruction are but a few of the many strategies that are appropriate for use with students who learn at a faster pace. In order to be substantially challenging, classes must feature content and choices that are significantly beyond what typical students are offered. Without this pairing of characteristic and program design, a class is inappropriate for the students who learn at a faster pace.

The second defining characteristic of students in need of differentiated programs is an ability to learn in greater depth. Programs for students who display this defining characteristic are those that give students the opportunity to look at content through organizational structures including features such as interdisciplinary focus, complexity, and problem solving. Students, who are able to look at matters in greater depth, find appropriate service in program opportunities such as mentorships, independent studies, original research, and exchange programs.

Interests are the third dimension in which students of high ability differ from their peers. Students may have interests similar to older students or have interests that are unique (Achter, Benbow, & Lubinski, 1997). The unusual pattern of abilities and talents often translates into behaviors that make this characteristic apparent. Associated programs need to include opportunities to explore topics that are not in the traditional curriculum or are a different interpretation of the standard scope and sequence. Full-service programs might include subject-based seminars, minicourses, independent investigations, and service projects. The options are limited only by the imagination of the program planners and students who participate.

Zoo Apprenticeships: Finding Service in the Community

You won't believe the job I got for the summer. I'm going to work at the zoo and help with the penguins. I'll feed them their afternoon fish and make sure that they are not in any kind of danger from the visitors. I guess they have had instances when people have thrown coins into the water where the penguins swim. If they try to eat the coins, they can die. They said the money could block their windpipes or cause real problems with their stomachs. Can you believe it? I'm going to be an apprentice at the zoo! All I am being asked to do is keep a journal of experiences so that I can get my community service credit for graduation.

June 16th. Today was my first day as a zoo apprentice. I was really excited to get this job because I love animals and am hoping to be a veterinarian. I hope that I will be able to see how the zoo operates and go with the resident vet as she works with the various animals. Today they showed me the penguin exhibit. I actually was able to feed the penguins. Luckily they had gloves for me to wear. The fish were really fragrant!

June 24th. I can't believe I have been doing this apprenticeship for a week. Time has gone by so quickly. Dr. Minor is really terrific. She has let me do just about everything. I am in charge of the afternoon feedings of the penguins. They are a riot to watch as they all go after the fish they have for that meal. Dr. Minor has also taken me on rounds as she takes a visual inspection of the animals and their habitats. It is really interesting to listen to her explain what she is looking at and why.

June 30th. I am now in charge of the afternoon penguin feeding and 1:15 show. It isn't a show in the conventional sense as this zoo thinks such shows exploit the animals. Rather, I am the one who tells visitors about the penguins, what they eat, the different types of penguins, and how the zoo maintains their environment. The macaroni penguin is my favorite. They make me laugh each time I see them jumping from the water onto the side of the pool. Dr. Minor has a tough job. Maintaining all the zoo animals keeps her busy, but she says she likes the variety of problems she faces. I can't get used to the nocturnal Australia exhibit and its *bats*!

Students display these characteristics in various combinations. Thus program designers must assemble options that include a wide range of possibilities. Challenge, variety, relevance, creativity, flexibility, potential for decision making, and problem finding are among the features of programs that might be amassed in preparation for assembling a program mosaic for this population.

To Mr. Spence, this concept complemented his understanding of MI, multiple abilities, and multiple outcomes to learning. A complete cognitive shift took place that would fundamentally change his outlook on learning: "AHA! Not only do the more adept learners vary on these factors—all children vary in this way. Of course . . .

■ DEVELOPING PROFILES OF ABILITY

This new idea was so encompassing, Mr. Spence had to stop and absorb its dimension. People learn differently. The capacity to learn varies in each person. The methods used to learn must also vary. If maximum learning is to take place, variety must be present in the activities and events that shape the learning experience. It seemed so fundamental that he was surprised the pieces had not come together long ago.

In order to accurately match students to the programs that will correspond to their learning needs, POAs are a useful guide (see Figures 2.1 and 2.2). These profiles (Parke, 1989) are forms upon which program planners can summarize essential information needed to make matches to existing programs or recommendations for programs that are needed. The actual content of the POA may vary based on the priorities of a given school or district but will essentially contain similar information types. These include student name, grade level, date of profile, pertinent assessment information such as student products and competitions, student-completed interest inventory results, teacher recommendations, parent inventories, and anecdotes collected from people participating in the process. An area for placement decisions and evaluation data should be reserved. It is likely that these profiles will need to be updated on a regular basis and can easily be integrated with portfolio assessment activities. These standardized profiles become the source of information from which program and placement decisions can be made.

Michael is a fourth grader interested in science. For the school science fair he had developed a working model of the locks at Sault Sainte Marie that separate Lake Huron from Lake Superior. He demonstrated how the locks allowed boats to go from the higher lake (Superior) to the lower lake (Huron) without having to go down treacherous waterfalls. The project was based on a law of physics that water reaches its own level. The depth of knowledge evident in the project presentation was unusually insightful for a student his age. In fact, it was so well executed that his project was displayed at the regional science fair.

Information gleaned from Michael's participation in the science fair is exactly the type of data that should be recorded on a POA as it tells a great deal about him as a student and person. He is interested in science and physics in particular, is capable of reasoning at a level that exceeds his age peers, completes work on time, and, as directed, is orally proficient and is self-directed in his learning. These data provide program planners with essential information to make further decisions about what types of programs fit Michael's profile. Options such as the Work-School Exchange

Figure 2.1
Sample Profile of
Ability (Elementary)

Name: _Mark Tunny_		School: _Cedarville Elementary_
Address: _113 Pike Place 47628_	Grade: _3_	Date of Birth: _10/24/93_
Parent Name: _Jennifer Tunny_	Phone: _245-9900_	Date of Completion: _10/23_

Assessment Data:*

Test/Assessment	Score	Date
California Achievement Test–		
Reading Comprehension	9 stanine	4/18
Vocabulary	9 stanine	4/18
Teacher Recommend (Gr. 2)	Top 1%	5/18
Teacher Recommend (Gr. 3)	Top 1%	9/9
Interest Inventory (Gr. 2)	Reading	5/24
	Writing	5/24
	Crafts	5/24
	Swimming	5/24

Placement Decisions:	Effective Date:
Young Authors	1/7
Cross Grade Grouping (to 4th)	2nd Quarter

Evaluation Data:	Effective Date:
Begin with placement:	11/15
Grades	
Interview (student, parents)	
Checklist–program teachers	

Signatures: Alice Newcomb, Program Coordinator
            Jennifer Tunny   Mark Tunny

*Norm-referenced tests, criterion-referenced tests, inventories, products, competitions, nominations. *Please write anecdotal information on back of page.*

Day, and the Summer Institute at the Shore (sponsored by the local Community College) are apt for this student.

Sean, a kindergartner who came to school reading, provides another example. His parents reported at the prekindergarten screening that he had been reading for over a year. They described how they have read to him each day since he was a toddler. He regularly selects books as a form of entertainment and is particularly fond of picture books and easy-reading books. Eric Carle, Marc Brown, Katherine Holabird, and Margaret Wise Brown are among his favorite authors. On trips to the library, he always looks for books by those authors first. How well his parents remember the day when Sean was sitting down with a new book, *Does A Kangaroo Have A Mother, Too* (Carle, 2000). His Mom related that she heard him using the pictures to tell the story . . . or so she thought! When she looked over Sean's shoulder, she found that he was reading the exact words on the page, with no help and no mistakes. Sean is a spontaneous

Figure 2.2
Sample Profile of
Ability (High School)

Name: _Tina Attwood_   School: _Athens High School_

Address: _1648 Sanger_   Grade: _12_   Date of Birth: _8/3/85_

Parent Name: _Ian Attwood_   Phone: _776-0041_   Date of Completion: _8/19_

Assessment Data:*

Test/Assessment	Score	Date
AP History	4	5/12
AP French	5	5/12
Overall GPA	3.92	6/15
French GPA	4.2	6/15
History GPA	4.0	6/15

Placement Decisions: Effective Date:
Dual Enrollment – WCCC   Fall Term
French
Lincoln Museum Apprentice   Fall/Winter Terms

Evaluation Data: Effective Date:
Begin with placement: 8/30
Interview (student, parents)
GPA

Signatures: Kathryn Bach, Program Coordinator
Tina Attwood   Ian Attwood

*Norm-referenced tests, criterion-referenced tests, inventories, products, competitions, nominations. *Please write anecdotal information on back of page.*

reader with skills far advanced from his peers. It was apparent that in order to keep Sean interested in the kindergarten reading activities, his teacher would have to plan work that surpassed letter sounds.

It was obvious to school personnel, as well, that Sean would need supplemental programming, and so he became a POA candidate. Performance levels on school readiness and reading achievement scales were recorded along with anecdotal information from his parents, the classroom teacher, and the school librarian. An interview with Sean was also conducted focusing on his interests in book topics, types, and authors. Interview was the chosen format as Sean's writing skills were far less developed than his reading skill.

During a follow-up interview, Sean's classroom teacher reported that she had already added more advanced books to the classroom library for Sean and other students to enjoy. She was also having him read favorite books to the class or small groups of classmates. She indicated that Sean was writing some but not proficiently. His writing and spelling were similar to that of kindergarteners. With the amassed POA information, the decision was made to talk to Sean's parent as well as Sean, to suggest he travel to a first grade classroom for reading. They were told that this recommendation was being offered as the pace and depth of his reading was obviously faster and deeper than that of the other kindergartners. Not only would he be reading at a similar level to the first graders, his POA indicated that he also had the academic and social skills needed to successfully participate in other reading activities.

DEFINING CHARACTERISTICS AND PROGRAM DEVELOPMENT ■

With POAs as an underpinning, a talent development model can become a strong component of educational programming. VanTassel-Baska asserts, "The case could be made that all of education should be about talent development" (p. 761). The spectrum of abilities revealed on the profiles becomes a guide for program development. These can be translated into the language indigenous to the MI model or other models such as Autonomous Learner (Betts, 1995), Schoolwide Enrichment (Renzulli, 1994a), Talents Unlimited (Schlichter, 1997; Taylor, 1968), or *The Parallel Curriculum* (Tomlinson, Kaplan, Renzulli, Leppien, & Burns, 2002).

Treffinger (1998) outlines a talent development model particularly well suited as a partner to the concept of program mosaics and POAs. The model, Levels of Service (LoS), is based on three fundamental principles. First, talent is generated through the combination of four parts. They are the *characteristics* of the student, the *context* in which the student is placed, the *content area* in which the student is involved, and the *operations* or *tools* the student uses to create products. The resulting service delivery system differs from those traditionally used in gifted child education in these four ways (see Tables 2.2 and 2.3).

Unique to this model is the manner in which talent development is translated into program structures. Four levels are defined with all students being included to some degree. Students with more typical abilities are eligible for service in levels 1 and 2 (Services for All and Services for Many). These differ in that level 1 is ongoing and is an integral part of the general-education program structure. Archaeological digs, community service, reenactments, and the Young Authors program typify level 1 activities. Level 2 is made up of optional programs (such as 4-H, Junior Great Books, and band) that students can self-select based on their interests, and program availability, and scheduling. Level 3 is the point at which programs require more unusual levels of talent. Students are eligible for programs at this level when their abilities significantly surpass their age peers. At this point, then, options beyond the typical general-education programs are necessary to fully develop the students' abilities. For admittance to such programs, students must meet eligibility guidelines. Programs at level 3 might include Advanced Drawing Seminar, All-City Choir, Discovery Seminar, Mental Math Competition, or AP Chemistry. Level 4 programs are reserved for the highly talented students. They require students to be so far beyond the norm that programs that appropriately suit their POAs are unusual for the general education scope and

Table 2.2
Summary of LoS
Model

Typical Programs for Gifted	LoS Model
Acceleration and enrichment programs available for students	Individual program decisions based on student strengths, talents, and interests
Based on set of predetermined abilities	Based on unique characteristics of each student
Identify "truly gifted"	Identify strengths, talents, sustained interests
Serve percentage of students	Serve all students to some degree
Inclusion vs. exclusion	Designing appropriate programs for all students
SOURCE: D. J. Treffinger, 1998. Used with permission.	

Table 2.3
Programs and LoS

Levels of Service (LoS)	Corresponding LoS Program Characteristics
Level 1: Services for All Students	Appropriately challenging programs are for all.
	Occurs in general education classroom daily.
Level 2: Services for Many Students	All may participate in options available. Students select based on interests, options, and availability.
Level 3: Services for Some Students	Eligibility is by evidence of skill level and qualification.
	Students are placed in programs that significantly extend and deepen specific talents.
Level 4: Services for Few Students	Eligibility is by evidence of extreme talent. Programs are very challenging and emphasize original research and productive thinking.
SOURCE: D. J. Treffinger, 1998. Used with permission.	

sequence. Such opportunities as dual enrollment between high schools and universities, original research, flex classes (see Chapter 5), and intense independent studies qualify as level 4 programs. Options at all levels are necessary and equally important. Creative programming may be necessary to develop options responsive to the wide variance of student need, particularly at levels 3 and 4.

It should be noted that the talent development paradigm, as described by Treffinger (1995), includes a variety of courses attuned to the variety of characteristics, needs, and interests displayed by the typical classroom mix of students. Some are more adept than others, and interests certainly vary. A student talented in one area may not be as talented in another. This variation leads conclusively to the position that full service for talented students must be a mixture of opportunities that correspond in some way to the students' individual profiles. Challenging options must be included as there are students capable of extending already-advanced talents even further. Programs requiring complex and sustained thinking are necessary as talent development requires employing and extending such skills.

These difficult courses are a fundamental component of maximizing talent (Clifford, 1990). Gagne (1995) points out that intensity grows as level of talent grows. Basic programs are also essential under the talent development model. They strengthen general education programs and provide the differentiation rarely available for high-ability students in the regular classroom environment (Westberg, Archambault, Dobyns, & Slavin, 1992). Program planners are cautioned to keep in mind that more fundamental programs do not replace those for students who display unusual talent or precocity (Feldhusen, 1994).

TALENT DEVELOPMENT ■
AT GREENWOOD MIDDLE SCHOOL

Up to this point, Greenwood's school district made curricular modifications as deemed necessary. The district had a strong program based on the state's many content standards and a carefully crafted curriculum alignment. Unfortunately, the required course structure left little time for extras. A decision had to be made. Is using talent development as a guide for program development fundamental or is it a time-consuming add-on that really is not within the boundaries of what the district can justify?

Mr. Spence considered the question and came to a decision:

> Many pieces of a talent-based program are already in place. But there are obvious holes, as Sophie's situation points out. One of our priorities must be to formalize a mosaic of programs that can be matched to students' abilities, possibly based on POAs. If we do it correctly, the task may result in a stronger education for all of our students. I am certain that we can do this.

Mr. Spence was naively optimistic. For if it were easy, all schools would be far closer to the ideal. As it is, there are more pitfalls than one can imagine, and each has the potential of putting a program off course. Mr. Spence had a conception of what a comprehensive program should look like. He felt confident that the board of education would be willing to put policy in place that would outline the steps needed to reach the goal of differentiated programs based on students' talents.

His next step became all too apparent with the arrival of a referral to the special education department of a student with problem behaviors. William was a student who was having trouble making the transition to middle school. His acting-out behaviors had escalated from controllable, attention-seeking behaviors to threatening interactions that jeopardized his safety and the safety of his schoolmates. A meeting of Greenwood's Intervention Team was scheduled to discuss the case. Mr. Spence, as principal, was part of the meeting, and what he heard further challenged his understanding of what a talent development model would mean for Greenwood Middle School.

William's meeting was quite normal and closely followed the established protocol for such referrals. What galvanized Mr. Spence's attention was a question posed near the end of the meeting by his special-education teacher and student advocate, Mr. Fruth:

What abilities does William display that are on the positive side of the ledger? It seems to me that he submitted a short story to the contest held by our evening newspaper, the *Monitor*, and it received an honorable mention in the middle school category. Am I right about that?

He was absolutely right. The next meeting of the intervention team was scheduled to study the case and formulate intervention recommendations for William's teachers. To get a complete idea of William's abilities, the team took Mr. Fruth's observation as a challenge. They set about developing William's POA. This required the completion of assessment instruments that would chart his strengths as well as weaknesses. Strengths could then be used to develop areas that were less strong. Again, Mr. Spence had an insight:

"Why not develop POAs for all our students?" was the question Mr. Spence posed at the next Curriculum Committee meeting. "If we could begin the process of gathering information about students' academic and nonacademic abilities, we would be able to determine if modifications are needed in our general-education program. We might even be able to get a reading on whether or not a talent development model is feasible for us. I have a nagging feeling that this may be complicated. But I am convinced that we should study the possibility."

The curriculum committee knew full well that once Mr. Spence had an idea in his head, change was in the offing. He promised to return to the next meeting with ideas and resources for study. The project came together as he distilled his thinking down to a written plan. He titled the project, "Greenwood Ability Profiles" (GAP). He was pleased that he had found a clever name for a program that reinforced his desire to close any gap between student needs and program offerings. He decided that the next step was to think more about talent development and see what could be done to gather support for this all-encompassing project that was sure to change the status quo. The GAP Group was assembled.

To Mr. Spence's surprise and delight, he found not only support among his staff members but also available resources to give direction to his research (Parke, 1995). Simply put, he asked himself this question: "In what ways might we determine the strengths and weaknesses of our Greenwood students?" Brainstorming this question, he came up with many ideas. Among the options were interviews with parents, teachers, and students; academic and interest inventories; videotapes of performances; portfolios of work products; tests; and observations.

With William's case pending, Mr. Spence approached the Intervention Team and asked if they would consider using some of the assessment options gleaned from his search as part of William's review. Luckily, they were more than happy to oblige as long as the measures gave pertinent information about William without extending the review beyond what was considered typical.

Concurrently, he spoke with other district principals, the school psychologist, and Mr. Fruth and was able to outline his ideas and collect sample assessments that could be used or adapted to serve the needs of the

Figure 2.3
Sample Interest
Inventory (Middle
School)

Name: *Elizabeth Lewis*   Teacher: *Mr. Janus*

Grade: *6*   Date: *9/25*   School: *Leo Middle School*

---

1. What is your favorite subject in school? What is your least favorite subject?

   Reading   *Science*

2. What are your two favorite books?

   The Witches and the Left Behind series

3. What activities do you most like to do on the weekends?

   Play basketball and be with friends

4. When you study, on which subject do you start? Why?

   Social Studies because I like to learn about history.

5. If you could invite a famous person to dinner, whom would you invite? Why?

   Albert Einstein because he is very intelligent

6. What do you wonder about?

   What heaven is like

7. Would you rather read directions for building a model airplane or have them explained to you?

   Read

8. If you could choose a project to develop for fun, what would it be?

   Make a tree house

Intervention Team. When the Intervention Team next met, they jointly decided to keep this first assessment simple and agreed to use an interest inventory (see Figures 2.3 and 2.4).

They also used a profile based on the MI model and an inventory of William's abilities in the visual arts and poetry writing (see Tables 2.4 and 2.5). These were chosen as William showed a proclivity in these areas, and they could easily be added to the assessment protocol typically used in the Intervention Team's data-gathering process. Mr. Spence suggested they use Detroit Public Schools' inventories called the Creative Product Scales (CPS) (Parke & Byrnes, 1984). They were in hand and could be completed without delay. The committee gave enthusiastic support, and the pilot went into effect.

William's scores were higher than expected on the CPS, making an interesting comparison to the other, more-conventional achievement measures that were used. His art, as assessed by the CPS and interpreted by the head of the art department, was determined to be quite precocious. His poetry, assessed by the CPS with scores interpreted by the middle school English teacher, also revealed William's skills to be surprisingly strong. It seemed that a useful addition to the assessment process had been found. The team carefully moved to the teacher recommendation stage of the intervention process, basing many suggestions on data gleaned through the use of the piloted assessment measures.

Figure 2.4
Sample Interest
Inventory (High
School)

Name: *James Hammerhill*   Homeroom Teacher: *Ms. Lee*

Grade: *10*   Date: *11/26*   School: *Bryan H. S.*

---

1. What is your favorite subject in school?

    Any science

2. What are your two favorite books?

    Anything science fiction and Hawking's <u>The Universe in a Nutshell</u>

3. What activities do you most like to do on the weekends?

    Work on cars and build robots for robot wars

4. When you study, on which subject do you start? Why?

    Anatomy because I understand it and I can finish it quickly

5. If you could invite a famous person to dinner, whom would you invite? Why?

    The President because I would like to talk politics

6. What do you wonder about?

    What the world will be like in 2035

7. Would you rather read directions for building a model airplane or have them explained to you?

    Read definitely

8. If you could choose a project to develop for fun, what would it be?

    My robots

9. What subject would you like to eliminate from your schedule?

    Gym!!

Master teacher and Intervention Team member Ms. Marge immediately noticed the pilot's success: "This has been a very useful exercise. Not only did these measures give this intervention a positive tone, they also may be interesting to the GAP group. Do I have your permission to share the intervention findings and tools?" The team gave permission, and the GAP Group began the process of developing POAs in earnest.

Sophie's mother was delighted when a parent inventory arrived in the mail. Not only was she more than happy to be part of the assessment process but she also learned a great deal about her daughter and the attributes needed for success in the programs for which she was being considered. It was surprisingly obvious from the items in the science section of the inventory that this was not an area in which Sophie would excel substantially beyond her classmates. The items chosen to reflect aptitude in science were not representative of Sophie's abilities in the least. While she was an excellent student of science, the items were geared toward discovering students that performed at an even higher level of ability than Sophie. Sections dealing with the arts and mathematics were another matter. It appeared to Mrs. Richardson that her daughter would be a prime candidate for inclusion in programs measured by these areas, as the

Criteria for Judging Poetry

Work: _____   Rater: _____

Rate each poem according to these 10 criteria. Indicate to what extent the work meets the criteria according to this scale.

1	2	3	4	5	6	7	8	9	10

To a very limited extent	Somewhat	To a great extent

1. The poem makes good use of *standard structural poetic devices.* _____
2. The poem sounds good *rhythmically* when read aloud.   _____
3. *Sound devices* such as alliteration are effectively used.   _____
4. The poem employs *striking images* or *metaphors.*   _____
5. The *diction* of the poem is appropriate and effective.   _____
6. *Irony and paradox* are well used.   _____
7. The poem goes beyond what might be expected in terms of *form or content.*   _____
8. The poem offers a *new* insight into a meaningful issue.   _____
9. The poem displays *intensity of imagination.*   _____
10. The poem has at least one *memorable characteristic* that will draw the reader back to it.   _____

Comments: **Total Pts.**

Table 2.4
Creative Product Scale for Literature, Poetry (Detroit Public Schools)

inventory items seemed to reflect the level of her talents and the activities in which she is most interested. To the GAP Group's delight, they were able to get valuable information from parents while educating them as to the characteristics needed to successfully achieve the goals of advanced programs. Complaints dropped dramatically, and parent representatives were immediately asked to join the GAP Group.

In his report to the assistant superintendent for instruction, Mr. Spence wrote the following:

> During the spring term, the GAP Group has made substantial progress in developing POA measures that were flexible enough to use widely throughout the district. The GAP Group, composed of classroom teachers, specials teachers, the psychologist, two parents, and an administrator, based the development of the POAs on

Criteria for Judging Art

Work: _____   Rater: _____

Introduction: While it's relatively impossible to evaluate an art product with objectivity, the following group of elements and principles of art should transcend cultural, geographic, sex, and age barriers as grading tools. They are absolutes which may appear in total or in part of a painting, sculpture, or craft product regardless of the sophistication of the producer. Consequently, a Leorardo Da Vinci, a Papuan native, or a Cass Tech art student are all aspiring toward the same composite ideal of elements and principles while expressing their individual concepts.

The evaluator should be forewarned that the number 10, or unique category, is synonymous with masterpiece and should therefore be used with cautious reservation. A masterpiece can only be rendered by a master artist, the work has to be universally recognized, it must have a life of its own, be technically perfect, comprise past, present, and future tendencies, and have staying power. Any additional comments you wish to make please, put them on the back of this sheet.

		DEVELOPING			ADEQUATE		COMPETENT		EXCEPTIONAL	UNIQUE
1.	UNITY	1	2	3	4	5	6	7	8	9	10
2.	LINE	1	2	3	4	5	6	7	8	9	10
3.	SHAPE	1	2	3	4	5	6	7	8	9	10
4.	VALUE	1	2	3	4	5	6	7	8	9	10
5.	VOLUME	1	2	3	4	5	6	7	8	9	10
6.	FORM	1	2	3	4	5	6	7	8	9	10
7.	TEXTURE	1	2	3	4	5	6	7	8	9	10
8.	COLOR	1	2	3	4	5	6	7	8	9	10
9.	CONTRAST	1	2	3	4	5	6	7	8	9	10
10.	HARMONY	1	2	3	4	5	6	7	8	9	10

Average Rating =

current practice and resources easily obtainable or currently used in this district. We know that the more our educational community is familiar with the measures used, the more widely accepted this new system will be. While we have confidence in the POA process, we understand that finding and developing additional assessment measures will be difficult. However, the outcome of being able to match student abilities with program offerings is an opportunity we can and shall meet.

In the upcoming term, our group will take on an even more daunting task. The GAP Group is set to do an inventory of

Task	Person Responsible	Date Due/Completed
1. Develop mock POAs.	Janice	1/28
2. Identify department heads.	Robert	1/28
3. Write GAP questionnaire of extant programs.	Pat, Carolyn	2/26
4. Meet with heads to explain and distribute inventories.	Spence, Chair	3/12
5. Collect inventories.	Robert	3/19
6. Collate data.	Susan	4/3
7. Review data with GAP.	Susan	4/3
8. Present data to department heads.	Spence, Chair	4/10
9. Seek additional information from department heads.	GAP Group	4/17
10. GAP meets to review outcome of meeting.	Spence, Chair	4/24
11. Write report of findings.	Judy	5/15
12. Submit to administrators.	Spence, Chair	5/27

Table 2.6
Project GAP Schedule for Developing Program Inventories

Greenwood's available programs so that we can determine the extent to which they match the mock POAs that have been created for this task. We anticipate submitting our findings and recommendations to the administrative staff and school board prior to the Memorial Day break. Hopefully, we will receive their approval and can begin using the POAs as early as fall. If there are any questions or concerns, feel free to contact any group member.

It was with great relief that the GAP Group received the news they desired. Administrators and board of education members enthusiastically embraced the project and its planned course. Wisely, they requested that a pilot be completed prior to districtwide implementation.

The committee was stunned when what seemed to be a clear road became quite the tangle. After a heated meeting, Mr. Spence and the group took a realistic look at the task at hand. First and foremost was the necessity to prepare a set of forms and formats on which all could agree. An ad hoc committee was appointed and charged with the development of an initial draft of each for the committee's consideration. The group framed that task using the wording, "Develop a document through which the GAP Group can compile information on students' strengths and weaknesses using the MI model and the defining characteristics of highly talented students." By the next meeting, a draft document was ready for review (see Table 2.6).

It seemed reasonable to begin the next phase of the GAP project with the review of the tenets they wanted to take forward. On each table were large pieces of paper and wide markers. Small groups assembled and began to brainstorm about the tenets in which they most believed. At the conclusion of the meeting, all voices had been heard and a preliminary list of tenets was agreed upon (see Box 2.1). Seeing the tenets on paper gave the group a new sense of direction. During each step in the implementation process, the GAP Group could look at the tenets and make sure all decisions were reflective of them.

Box 2.1   GAP Tenets

1. Intelligence has many facets that present themselves as individual differences.

2. Talent is found in many aspects of human performance.

3. It is the responsibility of educators to work with parents, teachers, and students to develop program options that suit performance differences found in their children and students.

4. The defining characteristics of highly talented students include the pace and depth in which they learn as well as their interests.

Table 2.7
GAP Program Matrix

Program	MI Area	Defining Characteristics		
		Pace	Depth	Interest
Film Festival	Linguistic Interpersonal Spatial	Students use film techniques that are advanced.	Students produce film entered in film festival.	Students select electives.
Mental Math	Logical Mathematical	Students study advanced content.	Students study and apply math principles preparing for county competition.	Students attend after-school activities.
Medical Mentoring	Logical Mathematical Interpersonal Intrapersonal	Students work on-site at medical center at early age.	Students witness the complexity of medical science and care.	Students apply or are nominated for program.
Adopt a Highway	Ecological Interpersonal	Students study ecological impacts of littering.	Students gain community awareness and understand volunteerism.	Students are in club project and volunteer opportunities.

In preparation for taking the project public, they had to iron out other matters and clarify the process of matching programs to POAs. Mr. Fruth again brought forth an idea that became most useful to the group. To make this task as simple as possible, he proposed a two-dimensional model that combined the notion of MI with defining characteristics. It was essential to prominently display the defining characteristics because they brought credence to the model. As pace, depth, and interests were the easiest categories to understand by the varied constituencies of the program, the group chose them as the descriptors for defining characteristics. Blending the defining characteristics within the MI framework gave the program planners the road map to differentiate curricular practice and design (see Table 2.7).

Luckily, it was not the most complicated of tasks. With the format in hand, the search for programs began in earnest.

CONCLUSION ■

Talent development is a process through which instructional options are combined into a program mosaic to which students are matched based on their talents and needs (Fulkerson & Horvich, 1998). POAs are one format through which the talents of individual students can be recorded, giving program planners a basis for organizing program mosaics and matching student talents to programming options. Through a talent development structure, program options can be in place from which individualized programs can be assembled and student-specific schedules can be planned.

POINTS TO PONDER ■

- The focus of the gifted-child education field is moving toward a broad acceptance of the term *talented* when describing students of exceptional ability.
- The definition of intelligence is changing from one of a single factor to embracing the idea of multiple intelligences.
- Using a talent model for establishing programs for students of high ability yields more broad-based and varied constituencies and programs.
- The unusual pace, depth, and interests of high-ability students are the defining characteristics of this population.
- In a talent development model, POAs can be developed for all students, to reflect their strengths and weaknesses.
- These profiles give direction to program developers and parents as they match students to available program offerings or undertake program development activities.

3

Ten Telltale Signs of a Hidden Program

If all programs that appropriately serve the needs of talented students were easily identified, there would be a greater number of youth enjoying stimulating educational experiences. Unfortunately, this may not be the case (Cox, Daniel, & Boston, 1985; Westberg, Archambault, Dobyns, & Slavin, 1992). There are many opportunities throughout the educational landscape of any school or community that will strengthen the match between profiles of ability (POAs) and program mosaics. One only has to vigorously explore the nooks and crannies of each landscape to find the treasures that lie within.

Where does the search begin? What are the signs of hidden programs? Is there a map available to make discoveries more sure? Investigators need only to widen their sights toward the field of possibility and be willing to consider even the most obscure prospects. By asking the question, "Does this program serve talented students well?" the prospector can begin to see the shining program shards that can become part of the overall mosaic to which individual POAs can be matched.

To make this job more defined for the Greenwood Middle School GAP Group (see Chapter 2), Mr. Spence decided to develop a rating sheet (see Figure 3.1), based on 10 attributes through which the members could rate the viability of potential mosaic programs. Together, these attributes

Figure 3.1
Hidden-Programs
Rating Chart

Program Title: Minicourse Friday

Factor	Rating*				
	1	2	3	4	5
1. Students are active learners.				◈	
2. Students are involved in decision making.					◈
3. Students learn strategies for how to learn.			◈		
4. Teachers facilitate learning.				◈	
5. Cooperative/collaborative skills are developed.			◈		
6. Interdisciplinary focus is part of the curricular design.				◈	
7. Materials/resources are rich and far-reaching.			◈		
8. Products have real-world applications.				◈	
9. Multiple outlets for products are used.				◈	
10. Instructional process includes parents/community.					◈
Total Rating Points 39					

Rating Scale*

1 = Very little evidence
2 = Little evidence
3 = Somewhat evident
4 = Very evident
5 = Extremely evident

Comments: Great opportunity to bring in community resources. Check availability of Janet Opper for French, David Pierce for Computer Aided Design, Liu for Eastern culture, and Kevin for Touring Europe.

SOURCE: From Beverly N. Parke, GIFTED STUDENTS IN REGULAR CLASSROOMS, © 1989. Reprinted/adapted by permission by Allyn & Bacon.

described the type of programs they were to include. When the rating sheet was presented, the GAP Group, to a person, felt an overwhelming sense of relief. The rating sheet brought the entire task into focus. Surprisingly, it also enabled them to be more adventuresome in their investigating as it brought structure to a seemingly random identification process.

ITEM #1: STUDENTS ARE ACTIVE LEARNERS ■

Designing aerospace transportation models, analyzing pond water, living time lines, interning at a local medical facility, constructing block structures, and monitoring the mushers' trek across frozen Alaska during the Iditarod are all projects involving students in active learning. Participants are actually doing the work of the project. They are learning by doing, living the work.

For all students, but particularly those with talent, the act of doing becomes a great deal of the learning that takes place. Renzulli calls this involvement in "real world experiences" (Renzulli, 1977). His work supports the use of this type of activity and points out the concomitant focus on real-world consequences (see Item #8). It supports the position that for learning to be the most challenging and effective, it should be active and grounded in real life. If it is, the participants will experience a more intense and challenging adventure.

Intense and challenging would describe two of the drama productions Mr. Spence had seen in his 15 years as principal of Greenwood Middle School. The first was in an eighth-grade English class with 22 students enrolled. The teacher, Mrs. Burkholder, felt as if the outstanding set of students she had that year were able to handle producing and presenting a play. She was shocked but delighted when the students pushed to mount a Shakespearean play. For eighth graders, Mrs. Burkholder felt that was a bit too much. In retrospect, she was glad she acceded to the wishes of the students. The class selected *A Midsummer Night's Dream*, as it was light and lent itself to fun characterizations and easy modification of language and script. In committees, students designed backdrops, collected props, sold tickets, created programs, read lines, and produced a wonderful memory. No doubt that in the future, the production of this play would be gloriously recounted by the students. Then there was the other production.

Joel, Michael, and David were the only eighth graders in accelerated English a few years later. Being in the accelerated section of English meant the students were involved in reading, writing, and thinking about literature at a more complex level than the other eighth graders. The boys were full of humor and challenge toward each other. They competed in everything from number of books read to remembering baseball statistics for the entire American League. During their unit on Shakespeare, they, too, produced *A Midsummer Night's Dream.* With only the three of them to handle all the parts, it did not seem likely that this would be a project they would enjoy. Not only did they make the activity riotously fun but they also insisted on doing a reading for the fifth graders. It was arranged and was a resounding success. It will be a long time before those lucky enough to attend will forget Michael as damsel Hermia, Joel as an entire troupe of actors in the Interlude, or David playing the part of a fairy flitting from place to place. They brought energy, insight, understanding, and interpretation to a play many dread reading. Not only was the reading a success, it motivated the fifth graders to create readings of their own.

Active learning is an excellent way to discover, as well as nurture, talent. It becomes a primary method for delivering experiences to talented students that are appropriate to their needs and abilities. Active learning allows students to bring their own interests and expertise to the fore. They can be involved in their projects as deeply as they wish, as artificial barriers do not have to exist. It also allows students to experience activities that are challenging and advanced for their ages. They can dip into their creative talents and emerge with products that they will long treasure. Active learning allows students with exceptional talent to further develop its boundaries. The activity need not be designated as *gifted and talented, honors,* or *advanced* to be an appropriate program for the participants.

ITEM #2: STUDENTS ARE ■
INVOLVED IN DECISION MAKING

The second dimension on Mr. Spence's list asked the committee to determine the extent to which a given program involved students in decision making. He knew full well that this is a difficult thing for many teachers to manage; but he knew it was vital to the broadest development of students' talent. Taking responsibility for one's learning is an ultimate goal of the educational process (Parke, 1995). Whether it is picking up one's room, working as a lab assistant in chemistry, choosing electives to study, babysitting for one's younger siblings, or serving as a class officer, developing the ability to make good decisions is central to success. If taken to the ultimate extreme in a school setting, this challenge may adopt the appearance of the students being actively involved in how and what is studied. At home, it may take the form of selecting after-school activities (e.g., flute lessons, basketball, paper route, life guarding, walking the dog). In either setting, involvement in decision making is a central characteristic of activities that serve highly talented students well.

Contracts are an excellent way to engage students in instructional decision making. Some schools have gone beyond the usual teacher-student contract and use the format as the basis for a seminar. Students are accepted into the seminar for one term following the acceptance of their contract (see Figure 3.2) by a review board, typically composed of teachers, students, and an administrator. At that point, students enter the class with a self-generated plan for completing the specified activities about which they have contracted. A faculty person serves as guide in what is often termed a Seminar in Discovery.

While this type of seminar experience is mostly found at the middle school or high school level, building the skills needed for student decision making is readily developed in the early grades. Something as simple as allowing students to self-select books to read after their work is completed builds this skill. Use of contracts, independent study (see Figure 3.3), student-led Fun Friday events, and self-evaluation opportunities can begin to develop the analytic and evaluative skills used in instructional decision making at a young age.

When parents involve their children in decision making, these skills may be even further refined. Regular family meetings, selecting volunteer opportunities, choosing chores for the week, behavior contracts, and allowances all give family members the forum through which decision-making skills can be practiced. Decisions are made throughout the day. Learning the skills to do so with success is an ability that must be practiced.

As with other factors under discussion, involving youth in making decisions is beneficial to all. Again, these skills are not only for the talented or high achieving; everyone can find these opportunities beneficial to overall development.

Figure 3.2
Sample: Seminar
in Discovery
Application/
Contract

Name: _Steven Wieraub_

Grade: _10_   Term of Study: _Third Quarter_

Homeroom Teacher: _10-B_   Seminar Sponsor: _Baurer_

I am submitting this application for evaluation and possible acceptance into the *Seminar in Discovery Program*. I understand that if accepted, I will attend this seminar for one semester in lieu of the _World History_ class.

During the course of the term I intend to do the following:
Develop a demographic map of the school district

I expect to use the following resources:
Latest census data (2000)
Sampling in community
Talk to realtors selling in this area
City planners

As a culminating project/event, I intend to:
Develop a research report on study
Make demographic predictions for the next 10 years
Present findings to school board

Student Signature: _Steven Wieraub_   Date: _10/15_

I, _J. Baurer_ _____, agree to serve as the sponsor for this student. I agree to provide the following resources (time & materials):

_____

_____

Decision: | OK /2nd Quarter | **See comments on other side** ⟶

ITEM #3: STUDENTS LEARN STRATEGIES FOR HOW TO LEARN

Children and youth with a high degree of talent are often assumed to have highly developed skills in learning. It is taken for granted that they know how to structure a paragraph, use a thesaurus, outline a paper, listen effectively, use the World Wide Web for research, construct effective questions, and the list goes on. In truth, these may be the very ones who most need to develop lifelong learning skills (Olszewski-Kubilius & Limburg-Weber, 1999). Knowledge and wiles may give them the ability to show mastery when little skill has actually been developed. As they first come on an experience that requires digging for information, they may feel daunted by the task. It is essential that opportunities to learn the skills involved in the learning process not be ignored.

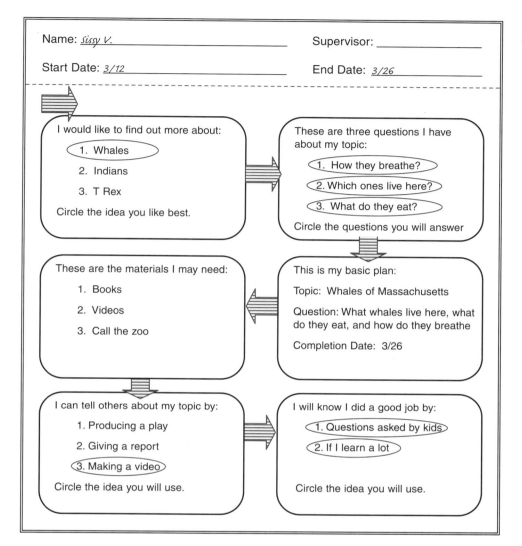

Figure 3.3
Sample: Elementary
Independent Study
Proposal/Contract

When K.C. was 7, he decided to investigate how a heart was constructed. He had always been intrigued by anatomy and read books on the subject when the opportunity presented itself. The librarian knew him by sight because he often sat on the floor in the science section with books twice his height piled around him. He could get lost in the reading and actually lose track of time and place. Everyone assumed that one day he would grow up to be a vet or a cardiologist.

That day nearly never came. K.C. was certain that he could talk forever on the subject, and his parents would have agreed. They heard story after story at the dinner table about the fascinating workings of the human body. Even at an early age, K.C. was invited to be part of a science fair sponsored by the local university. All agreed that he be given the opportunity to develop an entry for the fair. It took him no time at all to select the topic, "The Working Heart." He designed and assembled a cut-out model of the heart showing the auricles and ventricles. Blood vessels and arteries were clearly labeled. He was quite proud of what he had accomplished.

The day of the science fair came, and K.C. confidently assembled his project on the card table provided for his use. Behind the model, he had a stiff cardboard on which he tacked his report and some additional drawings. As part of the fair, he was expected to present his project and its associated report to a team of judges who would determine if the project merited a rating of superior, excellent, good, or incomplete. K.C. had no doubt that he would earn the highest rating and assumed his knowledge of the heart was unparalleled. He had refused to allow his parents or teachers to hear his written report prior to the fair. "Mom, I know what I am doing" was his mantra. While the adults were concerned, they decided not to push the point and let K.C. sink or swim. Unfortunately, when K.C. received a rating of excellent, he sunk. The judges' evaluation form noted that the model was terrific and the report complete. What they were not as pleased with was K.C.'s inability to clearly discuss his project during the question and answer period. He relied on what was written rather than being able to discuss the topic more informally. The judges were not certain that he had total command of the topic. Needless to say, K.C. was devastated. To him, anything less than a superior rating was a total disaster. He thought he knew the topic cold. Why hadn't the judges seen that? He vowed he would never enter a "stupid science fair" again in his life. "Science is dumb anyway!"

For K.C. and many others with high ability, holes appear in their learning even though they are seen as being highly accomplished. Too often, the holes become apparent, and the result is confusion and surprise. All of a sudden, the students question their ability or think there must be a mistake. Adults involved may think the child is not trying or is not so able after all.

Such situations can be easily avoided when strategies for learning (see Figure 3.4) are targeted. For K.C., a few trial runs of his project presentation would have prepared him for the judges' questions. Simple learning strategies are very valuable, even to those who appear not to need them. Including students in writing seminars, study skills tutorials, study buddy programs, computer-assisted instruction opportunities, or other programs of similar types can build skills as well as confidence. All students come to a point where intuition or present level of knowledge is not enough. It is then that mastering the structure of learning creates the ability to access the higher levels of skills and knowledge.

■ ITEM #4: TEACHERS FACILITATE LEARNING

It is no surprise that in programs that serve talented students well, teachers see their role as that of facilitator. Classrooms that focus on the teacher rather than the students are rare. Teachers of classes that stimulate talented students see themselves as facilitators, coaches, and guides.

In a classroom of this type, a number of differences are apparent when contrasted with more traditionally structured classes (Parke, 1989). Most important, the responsibility for learning falls on the shoulders of the students—not the teachers. Only the students can do their own learning. Teachers can set up the conditions under which learning takes place. However, it is still up to the students to do the actual learning.

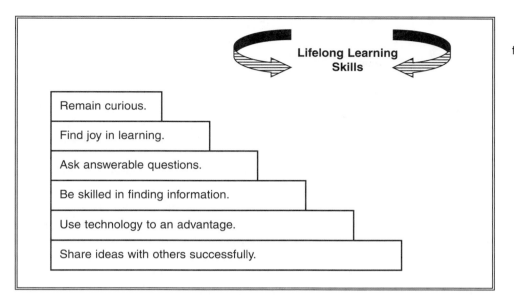

Figure 3.4
Strategies Needed
for Lifelong Learning

Teacher-Centered Classroom	Student-Centered Classroom
Seats always in rows	Seating suited to learning task
Bulletin boards not to be touched	Student-made bulletin boards
Everyone in seats at all times	Activity appropriate to task
Quiet	Reasonable noise level
Everyone on same page in text	Individualization apparent
Teacher decision making	Mutual decision making when possible

SOURCE: From: B. N. Parke, *Gifted Students in Regular Classrooms*. Copyright © 1989. Reprinted/adapted by permission of Allyn & Bacon.

Table 3.1
Teacher-Centered
Versus Student-
Centered
Classrooms

Thus these classrooms become student-centered—not teacher-centered (see Table 3.1). They often feature active learning, high levels of student participation, contracting, movement, discovery-based lessons, shared decision making, and other dynamic processes. Through this type of experience, students embrace the responsibility for their work. This is an essential skill for even the youngest of students.

Mr. Hyatt is a teacher who strongly believes in this philosophy of teaching. He sees students as resourceful people whom he guides in the discovery of biology. At times, he drives the high school administrators and maintenance people to distraction because his shelves are full of specimen bottles, and his filing cabinets are stacked to overflowing with all the tools of biological exploration. His teacher's desk can barely be found amidst the stacks of journals, equipment, and lab reports. The students find him a bit wacky but talk about his class to their parents and friends. Mr. Hyatt always has a little known tidbit of information to share with his students.

One of his favorite activities is to take the students down to the creek that flows on the outskirts of the school property and use it as an on-site laboratory for discovery. It is on the creek's shores that students develop their skills of observation, specimen collection and classification, scientific reasoning, slide preparation, and agility. Problems with the class do not include motivation. Extracting students from the site and getting them to their next class on time is a far more difficult task.

Through this type of teaching, students see the reason for developing the types of skills necessary for success in class. Class time spent on developing skills such as observation, classification, scientific recording, and reporting is economically spent as students see the need for these skills when they are in the field. The excitement generated in the course is in the application of skill development to exploration. Students do not study biology; they do biologically based scientific exploration.

Mr. Hyatt's class lends itself to exploration on many different levels. Highly talented students can create and report on a full scientific study using the creek as the laboratory. Students with lesser skill or interest can use the class as an opportunity to develop the basic skills of scientific exploration and hopefully an appreciation for the biological systems that surround us. For both types of student, and all those in between, the course is responsive to their level of development, and they can take the responsibility for building higher levels of knowledge and scientific skill.

■ ITEM #5: COOPERATIVE AND COLLABORATIVE SKILLS ARE DEVELOPED

One of the primary problems faced by students with unusual talent is that there are few students with whom they can mutually relate. Just by the nature of their defining characteristics, they differ from most of their age peers in that they may learn faster, have interests that are quite different, and comprehend what they learn in greater depth. Those distinctions often lead to feelings of isolation or superiority. It is, therefore, essential that programs in which students have the opportunity to work in cooperative and collaborative settings (Joyce, 1991) are included on the GAP rating sheet.

In these settings, one must develop the interpersonal skills that enable the pursuit of mutual goals. In order to successfully reach a goal, all parties must work together to complete the task. If there is true cooperation or collaboration, everyone has participated in the process, and no one has monopolized or abandoned the task. Group work can be difficult for those who are most talented. Conflicting points of view are recorded in the debate about the efficacy of using the cooperative learning model with high-ability students (Slavin, 1991). In a general sense, these students may see a direction they wish the group to take and may rebel if the group chooses another path. Some are consistently asked to be the leader and source of knowledge within the group and resist this role, saying they feel "used, resentful, and frustrated" (Willis, 1990, p. 8). They may even attempt to quit the group and go it on their own, citing the group's ignorance or unwillingness to listen to reason, preferring to follow their own vision. If allowed, the inability to work with others may set the students on a path to isolation as their unwillingness to develop the skills needed to work with others is reinforced.

One simple remedy for this situation is to include these students in cooperative and collaborative tasks from an early age (Feldman, 1986).

The ability to work successfully with others takes root in the home at a young age as children negotiate who will play with which toys, drink out of the blue cup, or sit on Dad's lap during bedtime stories. Sibling interactions such as these develop patterns for later use in interpersonal communication. Perfecting these skills early is a bonus for children but not always possible for those who are only children or children different from their peers.

Students with unusual ability are, by definition, different from age peers. How can they become proficient in the skills needed to work with others when it is not their natural inclination? The answer may be surprising. It may be necessary to actually teach interpersonal skills to this population. Focusing on the process of compromise is just an example of a skill needed when cooperating or collaborating. It is impossible to successfully navigate group projects without it. If a member of a team seems to hold on endlessly to one point of view to the exclusion of those held by other team members, a stalemate will occur. A stalemate makes reaching the group's goal impossible as it freezes all activity until compromise is reached. Without compromise, everyone loses, and emotions may explode.

When the Future Farmers of America (FFA) club decided to mount a seminar series of brown bag lunches at the high school, there were numerous matters that required planning. Content, date, time, and place were just a few. Even though they understood that trust and cooperation make a process much more fruitful, the planning committee could not agree on topics or speakers. There was a decided inability to finalize the plans. Jacob insisted that they invite a series of speakers to discuss the latest in chemical solutions to weed control. June was determined to have a series of speakers presenting ideas on saving the family farm. Robbie favored in-depth discussion of optimal barn configurations for drying crops. If each held onto the idea brought to the table, no plan would go forward to the overall planning committee. To advance, they had to find a way to agree on the content of the program. Without collaboration, the whole project would fold. The advisor to the club intervened. Using a simple problem-solving structure (see Figure 3.5), Creative Problem Solving (Parnes, 1977), she helped committee members use skills for decision making in order to resolve their dilemma. The program was soon finalized. A round table was designed in which participants could choose the topic most interesting to them, and all three FFA members were satisfied with the arrangement.

Constructing model planes was the hobby most enjoyed by the Everest children. Jimmy was 6 and Robin was 9 when their interest became quite intense. It took them 3 years to arrive at an understanding that they would have more success flying their planes if they cooperated rather than fought. It was in the summer of that year when they decided to enter a contest sponsored by the local model aviation club. Entrants were to fly their remote-control planes through a number of maneuvers. The winning plane would be the one under the most control during elaborate tricks. Both children jumped at the chance to show their talent in construction and aviation. They had only one problem. Each of their planes needed more than one person to handle the preflight setup. The siblings' competitiveness showed as they pondered from whom they should enlist help. Neither could even conceive of asking the other. It was not until they were unsuccessful in lining up assistants (their friends had long ago learned that they did not want to get in the middle of this rivalry) that it became

Figure 3.5
Key Activities
in Creative
Problem-Solving
Model

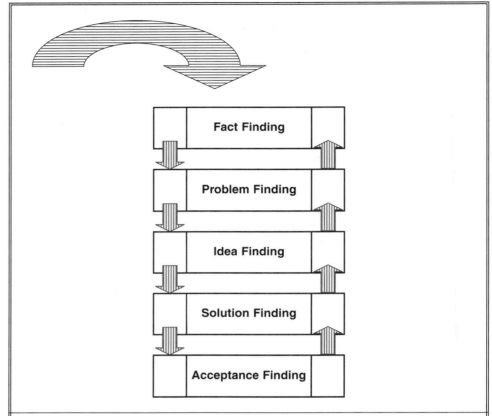

SOURCE: Copyrighted material from *Gifted Child Quarterly*, a publication of the National Association for Gifted Children (NAGC), 1707 L Street, NW, Suite 550, Washington, DC 20036. (202) 785-4268. www.nagc.org. This material may not be reproduced without permission from NAGC. Reproduced here with permission.

apparent that they either work together or not enter the contest at all. It was a painful decision but a necessary one. They would enter as a team with each one serving as crew (and silent at that) for the other's entry. While they did not win the competition, they did find cooperation was not as impossible as they had previously thought.

Purposefully including opportunities for developing collaborative and cooperative skills in a student's activities at home or school can have lifelong benefits. Everyone needs these skills to be successful, and it should not be assumed that those with exceptional talent already have them. It may simply be leadership skills, intimidation, or a strong personality that is on display. True cooperation and collaboration require the acceptance and trust of others. Experience builds these skills.

■ ITEM #6: INTERDISCIPLINARY FOCUS IS PART OF THE CURRICULAR DESIGN

With the talented typically being able to comprehend ideas in greater depth, they often see the complexity of relationships that lie at the center of most ideas, problems (Starko, 2000), and skills. Since this ability already exists and affects the way they think, it is for their benefit that hidden programs focusing on the interdisciplinary nature of life's systems (Miller & McCartan, 1990) are targeted for program mosaics. Not only will these programs sharpen their abilities to work in an interdisciplinary venue but they also teach the students to think (Piirto, 1999) and give the students a chance to broaden their range of expertise.

Team teaching is one structure that lends itself to the interdisciplinary perspective (Fogarty, 1995). When language arts teachers team with teachers of the social sciences, unique partnerships of knowledge may emerge. The social sciences can provide a context for the study of the language arts. Reading primary sources, writing letters, organizing information, public speaking, and conducting debates are among the skills that are developed in both disciplines. Merging the content of each into one dynamic course may result in outcomes that exceed those expected when the courses are taught separately.

Consider, for example, the study of the civil war when taught by Mrs. Pyne and Mrs. Lipnicky, team teachers of English and social studies at Greenwood Middle School. Students in their fifth-grade classes are involved in activities that are dynamic in their convergence of these two disciplines. Learning activities include reenactments; readings of letters from soldiers to home; map construction of primary battle sites; oral presentation of great speeches of the time, such as the Gettysburg address; term papers analyzing the basic philosophical positions of the Confederates and the Yankees; playing music of the time and analyzing how it reflects the political realities; and debates focusing on how history would be different if Lincoln had lived.

Such broad-reaching projects and learning opportunities are excellent means for offering challenging curricula appropriate for all students. Those with greater ability can easily take any one of the activities and develop a product commensurate with their capabilities. Those with more-typical abilities are able to do the same. Not only is there flexibility for differing depths of exploration but there is also unusually rich content for those students who find they learn more quickly or have interests that differ from their age mates.

The world is automatically, cognitively processed from an interdisciplinary point of view. It permeates growth and development of talented youth (Robinson, 2000). A family trip to the local children's museum can result in building understanding of many different disciplines. By reading the exhibit notes, calculating how many minutes until lunch, watching the stars move across a planetarium ceiling, walking through a giant model of a human ear, following a map to the Egyptian sarcophagus, or asking questions of the docent, myriad skills are being used. Developing them in such a natural environment almost disguises learning as an adventure.

ITEM #7: MATERIALS AND RESOURCES ARE RICH AND FAR-REACHING

Aquariums, World Wide Web, library cards, and a family dress-up box are all portals to discovery leading to understanding the world and how it

Figure 3.6
Suggested Materials
and Resources

operates. A never-ending mission toward meaning unfolds through books, television programs, conversations, and demonstrations that can lead to new ideas and meaning. So it is with children and youth. As they grow into adulthood, having access to resources and materials (Feldman, 2000) that stimulate thought can be critical to the process of learning (see Figure 3.6). Everyday objects, and those that are quite peculiar, can be a stimulus for activity. One never knows when the convergence of intent, possibility, and means will lead to a dynamic learning path.

For talented students, having access to as many different kinds of resources and materials as possible is essential to programming efforts that yield unique expression of meaning. Any tidbit, raggedy or pristine, can be a catalyst for new ideas and directions.

Kendra was a highly talented student with strong interests in two areas. One was in civics. She had been part of a city government-sponsored mentoring program throughout her high school years. It was her dream to be a big-city mayor or a state senator. Everyone agreed that she had the right mixture of attributes and brains to realize this dream. There was only one problem. She was also a first-rate painter who dreamed of having her work hang in the great galleries of New York City. Everyone agreed that she had the right mixture of attributes and brains to realize this dream, too. Kendra was 17 and had a world to discover and enjoy. She would lie in her bed at night wondering how she could be both. To be a viable politician took time and concentration. To be an accomplished artist also took a great deal of time and concentration. She wondered how she could commit enough of her time and energy to do justice to both. She saw that there were not enough hours in the day. It was only through her drive and the special opportunities available to her that she managed to develop both and put off that ultimate moment of favoring one over the other.

Kendra's mentoring program had been the highlight of her senior year in high school. Every Wednesday, she was one of a dozen students who job-shadowed members of city council. While she had an opportunity to work with up to 10 different civil servants during the academic year, she developed a particular bond with City Councilwoman Standish. Ms. Standish was young, vibrant, and very much involved in the issues that faced the city. She began the initiative to address the problem with brown fields in the city. It was also her work that brought a national software development firm to their area. She was always juggling what seemed to be a hundred things at once and doing so with the outward appearance of grace and calm. This amazed Kendra. She could see that the councilwoman had made many personal compromises to get to this level of city leadership. Her most current project was bringing an arts festival to their town. She had spent endless hours on the particulars as she developed a proposal to submit to the other members of council.

It just so happened that Kendra was assigned to work with Councilwoman Standish on a day when plans were really heating up. Phones were ringing, people were stopping by, and everyone wanted answers to their questions yesterday. Through all the chaos, the Councilwoman saw Kendra, at the adjoining desk, working on sketches for a festival poster. They were only in the shades of white, black, and gray but showed the excitement Ms. Standish wanted to convey. On the spot, she commissioned Kendra to design a fitting cover for the festival proposal. Given only a short time for development, Kendra still created the dynamic cover she had imagined. For that moment, her dreams of public service and art converged, and neither seemed as disparate as before.

Kendra was lucky to have this chance encounter as it brought her an opportunity to use both her passions on the same project. Being part of the mentorship program (see Figure 3.7) gave her the entrée she needed to take a giant step in her first-hand understanding of the workings of government and how it could be coupled with her passion for art and design. Granted, the occasions when she would be able to use both in the same pursuit were limited. That one opportunity, however, gave her the hope she needed to move forward toward her dual goals.

As it was for Kendra, it is for many people of all ages. Realizing one's potential is the hope teachers and parents have for all students. Bringing them in contact with the rich resources of the world, through whatever means, takes them a step closer to that goal (VanTassel-Baska, 1994). While being a packrat is less than an orderly existence, the excuse of, "You never know when you are going to need this," surprisingly rings true. For it is impossible to know when or what is going to turn on the light bulb in a person's brain that illuminates a whole new level of understanding what is and what can be. Rich and far-reaching resources and materials are one

Figure 3.7
Attributes of Mentors

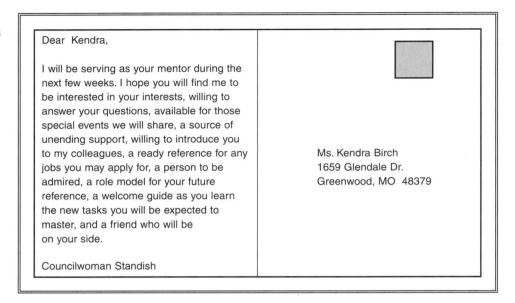

path toward creation and should be a consideration when identifying hidden programs. It matters not if these resources are found at school, home, online, in an attic chest, under a rock, or in the community. Most anything has the potential to be a fertile source of inspiration. Such richness should not be reserved for the talented few; it should be there for all to use in the development of their own creations.

■ ITEM #8: PRODUCTS HAVE REAL-WORLD APPLICATIONS

When asked to relate stories about their grade school and high school years, adults often talk about experiences they have had such as singing in the youth choir, answering questions as part of the quiz bowl team, running the 300-yard dash in gym class, making a critical first down in Pop Warner football, dressing up as Mark Twain for the third-grade play, or taking a senior trip to New York City. It seems that the most vivid memories involve active experiences. Entrenched, even decades later, are memories of times in which behaviors were open to public scrutiny. "What if I forget my lines?" "The whole sideline crowd is clapping for me." "Please do not let me miss this crucial quiz bowl question!" The mixture of activity and real-world evaluation of performance seems to lead to cherished lifelong memories.

This type of activity also leads to a deeper understanding of the performance guidelines that are set for every area of work. Whether specified or implicit, actions are subject to evaluation. At work, home, school, and play, performance is judged. It is that judgment that shapes the expectations of others and us.

EXCERPTS FROM: THE COOLEST CAMPING TRIP

By Jeff Merz, 4th grade, Leo Elementary

Ring, Ring! The bell was ringing at Lakewood Elementary School as class let out on Friday afternoon. Boy, I am as excited as a kid on the first day of school. Today is my twelfth birthday and I am going to Pokagon State Park tomorrow for my party. . . .

My name is David and I have wavy, blond hair and blue eyes. I guess I am a pretty nice kid except to my pest brother, Sam. I am also big on science. My favorite part of science is the hands on activities. That is one reason I love the outdoors so much, . . .

Because I love the outdoors, I know every trail in the woods in our addition. We live next to an area with sycamores, pines, and cottonwood trees. I have hiked with my Dad and Grandpa since I was a kid. And now, I know the trails by myself. . . .

My Dad said I could pick one friend to take along for the weekend and I knew in an instant who I was going to invite. It was my best friend, Josh Brent. . . . He is taller than I am which makes it easy for him to rebound the basketball over me. Also, he wears glasses, which kind of makes him look scientific and he has the same love of science that I have. . . .

So writes Jeff Merz, a fourth grade award-winning Young Author. *The Coolest Camping Trip* is the second of his books chosen to represent his school at the yearly regional Young Authors conference.

"I get my ideas from my real life experiences. I wrote this story because it really happened to my family. I changed the names to make it more interesting." Jeff is a writer by choice. He keeps a personal journal in which he writes two to three times per week. "I write if it is a bad day. I write if it is a good day. If it is a normal day, I don't usually write." he divulges. "When I write, I try to make myself better. Writing helps me set my goals."

Jeff has shown his writing talents in other forums. He has also received recognition from the county library system for his poetry. Jeff will find many topics to write about in the future as he is also a member of the swim team, runs the 4×100 relay for his class, and sings in the school choir. And now back to the story. . . .

I awoke to a buzz, buzz, buzz when my alarm clock went off. I jumped out of bed like it was a trampoline, pulled on my jeans and a tank top, and tied a light jacket around my waist. A quick breakfast was all I could handle—I was so excited! I jumped into the van and yelled for Dad and Sam to hurry up. . . .

We arrived at Josh's two story, brick house. It is my Mom's favorite house in the neighborhood because it has so many windows in it. She says if Josh's family ever moves, we would look at buying his house. Wouldn't that be weird if we lived in my best friends old house?. . . .

"Hi Josh," I said, "What's up?"

"A cool camping weekend and birthday party are straight ahead," he said. . . .

Finally, we reached the Pokagon State Park entrance. Dad signed us in and drove straight to our camp sight. We all looked for deer, but did not see any. The site was surrounded with gigantic sycamore trees, pines, and plenty of vines to swing on. . . .

Dad said, "Wow, the perfect spot!" He always said that when we pulled into a campsite! . . .

I grabbed some logs and put them by the fire pit in the middle of the site. Josh and I helped set up the tent. Then, put in our pillows, sleeping bags, blankets, and Sam's stuffed monkey. Was there going to be any room left to sleep? . . .

The group hiked up the hills, into valleys, around bends, and every spot they could explore. Sam got on our nerves. He sang every Barney song for half the trail. I think he walked all of us over the edge. . . .

Then the raccoons arrived!

SOURCE: Jeffrey Merz, Leo (IN) Elementary, 1999. Reprinted with permission.

Real-world application is a concept first brought forth by Renzulli (1977). It is his belief that high-ability students should be given the opportunity to try out their skills in circumstances that will yield real-world consequences. In that way, a greater understanding of the world and acceptable performance levels grows. Agreeing with this idea should lead the GAP Group into finding hidden programs that will give students a chance to learn more about themselves and their community.

The corner at Hillsworth High School (which Greenwood students attend) was a dangerous intersection. Not a year went by without serious accidents that were often life threatening. During the morning rush, student traffic was busy, as was the traffic into downtown. Both passed by this same intersection. Hillsworth students became more and more alarmed as the addition of extra warning signs, and traffic light turn signals did little to ease the problem.

It took the ingenuity of just a few students to make a major difference. As a class project, they were encouraged to conduct an on-the-spot survey of the traffic patterns at the intersection. After they analyzed the findings, they developed a plan for the safer travel of students and commuters alike. It was clear to them that it was necessary to take these findings and their plan beyond the project stage and submit them to the proper city authorities for review. At a meeting of the city's Safety Commission, the students presented their findings and plan. The Safety Commission took the plan under advisement and promised to study it further. All the participants were ecstatic when the Commission not only praised the plan but also allocated the money to make the suggested changes.

The next fall, Hillsworth students were grateful to see additional turn lanes as well as traffic lights that self-adjusted during hours of heavy traffic. The students were not satisfied, however. To determine the effectiveness of the changes, they continued their research and were relieved to find that the changes made by the city eased traffic congestion and resulted in far fewer accidents. Their real-world experience had resulted in real-life changes. This project was far more satisfying than designing plans that would be used only for classroom presentation.

Applying the notion of real-world applications of learning can easily extend to students at all levels of the educational spectrum (Renzulli & Reis, 1997). Preschoolers can contribute ideas when a new school playground is being designed. Elementary students can run the school store. Middle school students can submit poems to a literary magazine for youth. High school students can write weekly articles on school life for the local paper. The possibilities are endless and should not be limited only to the highly talented. It is this type of experience that serves all students well including those of high ability. Discovering the ingenuity of those students previously not seen as precocious is an added bonus of this approach to learning. The value of a program may stay hidden, but the participating students will not.

ITEM #9: MULTIPLE OUTLETS FOR PRODUCTS ARE USED ■

Independent study (IS) is a classic format through which students can develop projects on topics they find interesting. In most cases, students have the opportunity to select a means for displaying what they have learned. Among the products they may choose (see Figure 3.8) are models, diagrams, and written reports. This is a natural coupling of learning new concepts and projecting them to others in a meaningful way.

IS (see Figure 3.9) serves multiple purposes. Perhaps the most engaging is developing the ability to express oneself in many different ways. Being able to design a project appropriate to a topic is a skill in and of itself. Using an inappropriate means of displaying what is learned can lead to a project that does not show the content in the best light. Training for this skill, even at an early age, is done most effectively when students are given multiple means from which to select the manner through which they may show what they have learned.

When students are given a list of possible means for displaying what they know, they must use both analytic and evaluative skills to make the choice. These are considered higher-order thinking skills as defined by Bloom (1956). They actually take more time and brainpower to complete. Students are required to present new knowledge and to do so in a manner that is fitting. These skills may be difficult to develop, but they are easy for the teacher to require.

Figure 3.8
Products of Learning

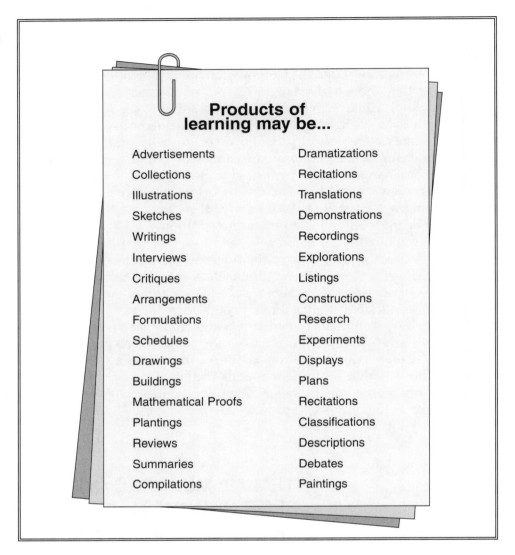

Part of the second-grade curriculum at Washington Elementary (which students attend before moving on to Greenwood) was a unit about Indian tribes. Students learned about the customs, territories, dress, dance, and ceremonies of the tribes. At the end of the unit, students were asked to select a project from three choices listed by their teacher, Mr. Miller. He also allowed them to submit a plan of their own design, after which he would make the judgment as to whether the proposed project was appropriate to the goals of the curriculum. For the unit on Indians, Mr. Miller gave students the choice of building a diorama of the area and its natives, writing a story about a typical day in the life of an Indian family, or creating a ceremony in which the different customs of Indian life were displayed.

For the most part, students were content with these options but not Sara. She preferred to generate her own ideas. In this unit, her interest was captured by the lives of Indian women. Mr. Miller agreed that she could design a project around this topic. Everyone in the class, including Mr. Miller, was intrigued by the pantomime she delivered depicting the roles native women assumed 300 years ago. Sara's work always showed more passion and insight when she focused on a project of her own design.

Figure 3.9
Independent Study
Proposal/Contract

Name: _____

Grade: _____ Beginning Date: _____

Homeroom Teacher: _____ Completion Date: _____

Questions I want to answer:

   1.

   2.

   3.

Resources I will use:

   1.

   2.

   3.

Projected activities and timeline:

   1.

   2.

   3.

Reporting options:

   1.

   2.

   3.

Evaluation options:

   1.

   2.

Highlight chosen options.

Student Signature: _____

Sponsoring Teacher Signature: _____

| Accepted   Revise   Rejected | *See Comments on Back of Sheet.* |

Mr. Miller found that Sara's skills in planning and executing her project ideas strengthened as she completed more studies. Success seemed due, in part, to the way his teaching strategy allowed her to explore her interests in greater depth. She and Mr. Miller made a good pair as they both found the other to be dynamic and challenging.

Students of Mrs. York knew by her reputation that she, too, was a fun but demanding teacher. Other students were constantly seeing Mrs. York's middle school math sections investigating one thing or another. It was a popular game to guess exactly what was going on. On this day, her students were digging up the turf just off the soccer field.

What they were witnessing was the latest of Mrs. York's math investigations. After dividing the class into three groups, she asked each group to predict the number of earthworms that would occupy a 36-by-36-inch area and to create a strategy to test their predicted answers to the problem. Three groups and three different strategies later, they set out for the destination required by their method of discovery. One group dug up the specified amount of turf and actually counted the number of worms they found in it. The second group dug up a 6-by-6-inch area from which they extrapolated the findings to the full dimension called for in the problem. The last group used the World Wide Web to find information about the amount of turf needed for earthworms and applied that information to the problem presented.

Mrs. York took the next step toward teaching the students mathematical judgment when she asked them to evaluate the procedures and findings presented by each group. The class then rank-ordered the strategies used and defended their ranking by citing the effectiveness of each. Not only had Mrs. York given students various ways to show what they had learned, but she also had the students reflect on their own work. They wrote in their math diaries about the problem and how they might go about solving the problem differently if asked to explore it again.

Having options to display what is known is an obvious characteristic of programs that suit the needs of talented students (Cline & Schwartz, 1999). Mrs. York's math sections were not considered advanced; yet talented students were able to further their understanding of math because the structure of the course allowed them to work on in-depth problems while exploring what was of interest to them. The projects used as part of Mr. Miller's unit on Indian life did much the same thing. He gave students a structure through which they could explore what they found enticing. Students were given the chance to design and develop products that reflected their own capabilities without compromise. They could read as much as they wished, explore interests in as great a depth as possible, and display their findings in a manner that was their own. By doing so, the students were treated to an enriched curriculum responsive to their individual needs. Accepting this strategy, the GAP Group discovered yet more hidden programs.

■ ITEM #10: INSTRUCTIONAL PROCESS INCLUDES PARENTS AND COMMUNITY MEMBERS

Too often it is assumed that in order for a program to have any merit, it must be part of the school's curriculum. This is hardly the case. One exciting way to discover hidden programs is to look to the community (see Figure 3.10). Many school districts sponsor community education classes. Colleges and universities sponsor opportunities for students to learn through a broad range of classes under the local school's aegis. Generally, program listings are distributed through the mail or the local newspaper.

Taking a look at what is offered can be very fruitful for the talented learner (Clark & Zimmerman, 1998), as many programs are hidden there.

French, drafting, bridge, the score of *Madame Butterfly,* volleyball, topiaries, virtual-reality programming language, lunch with a scientist, wills and estate planning, Chilean culture, gourmet cooking, and graphic design are among hundreds of options available in community-based educational experiences. While all may not seem appropriate for talented students, it is important to investigate before dismissing a class as too pedestrian.

A course in bridge, for example, seemed poorly matched to Janine, a 13-year-old with high ability and a penchant for cards. With a call to the program's sponsor, Janine was able to determine that the class was being offered to teach the more complex bridge strategies. She was told that it was ill advised for a beginner to take this class. However, if Janine were a member of the target population, she would be most welcome to take the course despite her age. Not only did participation advance the thinking skills she needed to acquire master points, it also taught her a recreational activity, which she could enjoy for a lifetime.

Local museums and libraries are also teeming with compelling learning opportunities for the talented. Art museums regularly offer classes for students in such areas as watercolors, collage, restoring oil paintings, history told through stained glass windows, and impressionist painters. Libraries may be a source of classes on genealogy, rare books and prints, and illuminations, among others. When such classes are of interest to the talented person, the opportunity to enroll in the class is highly prized.

Widely known, school-based programs such as Art Lady, Junior Achievement, Philosophy for Children, and Science on a Cart are but a few that are excellent but often unavailable without parental or volunteer support. Needed volunteers may even be students from a higher grade who have been trained to work with younger students in a particular program such as Junior Great Books, yielding great benefit to both parties.

By bringing parents and community members into the district's instructional process, Dr. Benson, Greenwood's superintendent of schools, was able to build a curriculum far more responsive to the needs of his K-12 population. Partnerships began with the monthly meetings of a group of concerned citizens he called his Community Forum. Initially, this group met to be a sounding board for new offerings proposed by Dr. Benson. It grew into an advocacy group for the district and a source of community-based initiatives. It was this group that first championed the community mentor program. They also were the founders of a dual-enrollment program with the local university, company sponsored classrooms, the Donate a Computer drive, and community mentorships. Dr. Benson received great response from the community's businesses, parents, and students as they developed a vital partnership, working for the betterment of all.

Community and parental participation in school programs can lead to a wide range of program offerings and extended support for the schools

(Text continues on page 53)

STUDENT COLUMNIST

Ben Ness*

Clarkston News 1/7/99

Poets and professional surfers alike have observed that time passes most swiftly when experienced in the presence of enjoyable circumstances. This axiom is supported by a countless wealth of empirical knowledge, the most recent of which is the sorrowfully concluding Holiday Vacation whose presence dwindles even as I type these thrilling paragraphs.

My break was occupied by engaging in fascinating pursuits while in the company of equally fascinating people, and true to form, it progressed with the speed of an irritated mongoose. So tomorrow I am faced with the grim prospect of returning to school, an event whose ominous arrival will be greeted by something short of ecstasy.

I anticipate that my peers will wallow in a similar state of depression. We have been given a taste of liberty, and my suspicion is that the experience will only heighten the usual restlessness with which most go through the academic motions.

A vicious, paroxysmal fury is eminent, one catalyzed by the nurtured juvenile consciousness awakening from its apathetic slumber to realize that school is not necessarily the most pleasurable way to spend fleeting adolescent hours.

"There is sunshine!" the tentative voices will exclaim, "and there is Frisbee, and there are gardens, so what in the world are we doing here?" Vital and yet often overlooked by students is the principle that our attendance in class everyday is absolutely voluntary. We are individual beings, wholly in charge of and responsible for our own actions. There is no military force thrusting a bayonet into our back, forcing attendance against our will. If so inclined we could all ditch high school, join the circus and nobody could stop us. We could frolic in the snow all day, forget our grammar, forget our arithmetic, forget our geography, and have a grand time.

But to do so would be terribly impractical. Patrons of fun though they may be, most of the fortunate scholars with whom I engage in conversation also have an ambition beyond the accumulation of pleasure. For most this leads to some logical concatenation of activities, a critical piece of which is education.

It is archetypal Freudian combat. There is a desire for instant gratification, but this is curbed by rational faith in the Epicurean idea that responsibility now will lead to a much greater gratification in the years to come. To be successful a student must recognize the value of learning and make whatever coinciding sacrifices this commitment entails.

Freedom is a salacious, tempting opiate. We must treasure it when granted, but cannot allow ourselves to be overwhelmed when there is greater success to achieve.

*Ben Ness is a student at Clarkston High School. His column alternates with a column written by Clarkston Community Schools Superintendent.

SOURCE: Reprinted with permission from the *Clarkston (MI) News.*

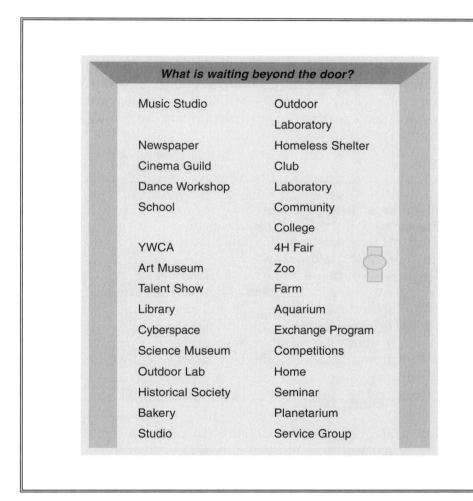

Figure 3.10
Places Programs
May Hide

(Betts, 1995). Outside the school walls, opportunities for talent development abound (Haroutounian, 1998). It is the wise program planner that harnesses these opportunities and brings them to the students who can profit from participation.

CONCLUSION ■

These 10 telltale signs of hidden programs are simply indicators of what may be rich experiences for talented youth. Signs may be found throughout the community and schools as hidden programs are found in even the most unlikely places. It is the clever program planner who has the insight to discover opportunities and then match them to the POAs of talented students. As more outlets for talent are found, the match between abilities and program mosaics can be more precise. It was the promise of this precision that resulted in the GAP Group's exhilaration as they could see the emergence of a wide array of opportunities for talent development.

■ POINTS TO PONDER

- There are many hidden programs that, when uncovered, can substantially enrich the development of talented students.
- An archive of program options should be continually compiled and updated so that program planners have the capability of quickly matching student POAs to programming options.
- Program planners should seek activities that show one or more of the 10 telltale signs of a hidden program that can benefit gifted and talented students:

---

1. Students are active learners.
2. Students are involved in decision making.
3. Students learn strategies for how to learn.
4. Teachers facilitate learning.
5. Cooperative and collaborative skills are developed.
6. Interdisciplinary focus is part of the curricular design.
7. Materials and resources are rich and far-reaching.
8. Products have real-world applications.
9. Multiple outlets for products are used.
10. Instructional process includes parents and community members.

4

From Hidden Programs to Inspired Programming

The final challenge facing Mr. Spence and the GAP Group was to find a way to ensure that the new conceptualization of talent development would become an integral part of the programming landscape at Greenwood. From past experience, he knew that programs in their beginning stages are often vulnerable to elimination or systematic disassembling. What could they do within the planning stage to make this initiative so much a part of the school district that it would not be in danger of cancellation? During a strategy session, the GAP Group created a plan based on the ideas of talent development, profiles of abilities (POAs), program mosaics, and partnerships with primary stakeholders. While understanding that vigilance was still a necessity, Mr. Spence was certain that the attention to these strategies would give Greenwood a defensible and comprehensive talent-based program for years to come.

PROGRAM MOSAICS ■

A program mosaic is based on the philosophy that in order to provide full service to students of high ability and talent, multiple programming options must be tied together in a model that contains programs that respond to the three defining characteristics of these students—pace, depth, and interests. Programs include those that are currently being offered in the district and community, hidden programs available in the district and community, and new programs that need to be developed in order to plug any holes that are evident after programs from the first two steps have been compiled. The more constituencies included in this assembly process, the more likely it is that programs will be identified that will strengthen the model and lead to the program's integration into the district's program offerings.

The program mosaic is made up of three primary pieces. The first is a panel of programs that allow flexible pacing for those students who learn at a faster pace. A panel of programs that encourages students to learn in greater depth is next. The last panel includes programs that are responsive to the students who have interests that are either more advanced from age or classmates or are unique to the general education population as a whole. These three panels merge to form a program mosaic that contains a spectrum of programs from which individual programs may be crafted from a student's POA. It must be pointed out that many programs span more than one area of the mosaic. Distinct categorization is impossible to achieve.

Pace Panel

Students of high ability are frequently identified through the pace at which they learn. It tends to be significantly more rapid than that of their age peers. These are the students who complete their work early or require little assistance when learning new skills. After completing their work, they may choose to read quietly or draw in a notepad. Surprisingly, they may also disrupt the classmates through antics resulting from boredom or disinterest.

Because pace is a dimension of high ability that is readily accepted and frequently observed (Rogers, 1992), programs that feature flexible pacing are likely to be a part of the current K-12 program offerings.

Grade Skipping

The commonly held conception of grade skipping, where students go from one grade level to a level higher than the natural progression (e.g., K, 1, 3, and 4, in which second grade is skipped) is a program configuration that can reasonably be included in a program mosaic. The inclusion of this option comes with suggestions, however. It is essential that all precautions be taken to make this transition as easy as possible for the students. When using this option, students who will be skipped should be functioning in the top 25% of the grade to which they are going and have sufficient maturity to successfully interact with the students in the receiving grade. This should minimize the danger of going from a very successful academic experience to one that is also likely to be successful but with challenge. It can be emotionally taxing for these students to enter an advanced environment in which they are at risk academically. The second suggestion is that the skipping occur when there is a natural change in the configuration of students, and new peer groups are being formed. This may happen at school entrance and, later in this chapter, is discussed under Early Entrance and Telescoping—or when students are changing buildings, such as the elementary students going to middle school or junior high school, or the middle school and junior high students beginning high school. In this case, a student who would typically be going from third to fourth grade might be placed in fifth grade at the middle school, skipping fourth grade altogether. This application of acceleration is not without potential complications and should be closely monitored by the parents and teachers of the accelerated student.

Early Entrance

For precocious 4-year-olds, early entrance to kindergarten may be a reasonable option. Typically, it is the parents who contact the school district and inquire if early entrance is a possibility. Some school districts readily use this option while others choose not to. If early entrance exists as a program option, parents are usually asked to have their children tested by an independent psychologist and have the results forwarded to the central administration of the district from which a decision will be made. Tests given for this purpose include achievement tests, aptitude tests, growth and development indices, and measures of maturity. As with any type of accelerated process that involves grade skipping or early entrance, students tend to acclimate best when they are projected to be in the higher levels of achievement within the receiving class. This is done in order to smooth the transition from one environment in which the students are achieving at a level higher than most classmates to a second environment where they are still a high achiever—but challenged. Hopefully, this will minimize any issues that may arise from the acceleration. It is also highly advised that students involved in an early-entrance program (or any accelerative process) be allowed to return to the original or similar program if the early entrance is not successful for the student. Please note that early entrance is also possible for 5-year-olds skipping kindergarten and entering school directly to first grade (see Table 4.1). In this instance it is highly recommended that the students have advanced reading skill.

Telescoping

Telescoping is a term used to describe another form of acceleration that can be used within a grade-skipping context. In this case, students are placed in a classroom that is mixed with students from two or more grade levels. Multiple-age groupings (e.g., primary Grades 1 to 3, fourth- and fifth-grade splits, or juniors and seniors in high school) also require content from many levels. For the highly talented students, usually but not necessarily academically talented, curriculum can be drawn from the skills targeted for the students in the higher age ranges of the class. Those students, then, join their older classmates when they are placed at the next highest grade or level (see Table 4.1). In this way, they are academically challenged, and the concern about losing a peer group is addressed as peer groups are shuffled with the new combination of students entering the new building or level.

Continuous Progress Curriculum

The program known as continuous progress curriculum is a building or districtwide initiative in which students work through the scope and

Table 4.1
Grade Skipping,
Early Entrance, and
Telescoping
Configurations

Configuration	Grade Levels
Grade Skipping	1, 2, 3, 4, 6, 7, 8
Early Entrance (5-year-olds)	K, 1
Telescoping	1, 2, 3, 4/5, 6, 7

sequence of the district's curriculum at their own pace. This process relies heavily on placement tests, curricular modules, a central organizational structure, skill groups, and a flexible teaching faculty. Students take placement tests frequently to determine their skill levels. They are then placed in curricular modules that feature the skills they need to develop. Skill groups and self-instruction are typical means through which students learn. Their skills are recorded in a format that is accessible to all faculty so that they can consult the latest records when planning instruction. Online program formats make this process easy to manage and available to the students and their parents.

It is easy to see that this type of structure is ideal for students who learn at a faster pace. They can work through the continuous progress curriculum and be involved with work that is at their skill levels rather than grade levels. There are limitations to this structure, however. Curricular opportunities must be available beyond the grade levels involved. Students highly talented in the academic or nonacademic areas included in the program may complete the skills for the students at the highest-grade level prior to reaching that level themselves. What do they work on at that point? This question must be addressed and resolved prior to implementation, for the circumstance will arise. In a situation where faculty members resist having students at lower levels study the skills introduced at their grade levels, controversy is likely. This is why the use of continuous progress curriculum is effective as a districtwide program supported by the administration and school board of education. Program planners should not see this as an elementary option only. Talented students need the continuous progress structure to continue to develop their areas of talent (be they languages, music, math, or design) across their school years.

Before adopting this program, policy makers must also address the matter of competency testing, as the school reform initiative has led to heavy concentration on passing the tests involved in school progress. This is likely to be far less of an issue for students of high ability as they generally meet and exceed proficiency standards with little effort. Typical students in the continuous program curriculum may have more difficulty with these tests if they are not able or motivated to handle the self-instructional nature of this program.

Curriculum Compacting

Renzulli and Smith (1979) designed a program structure through which students can work more quickly. It is entitled curriculum compacting. "In its simplest form, compacting consists of determining through formal and informal assessment procedures, the curricular content areas that some students have already mastered or might be able to master through modified approaches to instruction" (Renzulli, Reis, & Smith, 1981, p. 78). For students found to be advanced, they may skip curricular components they already have mastered or use formats of instruction through which they can advance more quickly than their classmates. Curriculum compacting offers a model that allows students to move through curriculum at their own pace, resulting in an acceleration option to the general education program listings and extra time for the student. They can then use the time freed from work already mastered to work on such activities as independent studies, other curricular skills, volunteering opportunities, science lab technicians, or computer-assisted learning. Thus curriculum compacting can be used for accelerating or enriching learning.

Self-Instruction

Self-instruction is a broad term used to characterize programs through which students can learn independently. These structures include provisions that allow for self-placement in an appropriate skill level, self-instruction of content, self-tracking of advancement, and self-evaluation of progress. Students of all levels can successfully use this strategy (Parke, 1983) when instruction is appropriately matched to the need and level of independent-learning skills. Programs are available through many systems of instructions. Computer assisted instruction (CAI) is one that has become readily available as computers have become commonplace in the classroom and textbook publishing companies have included these packages with textbook adoptions. Highly talented students can employ CAI to accelerate their learning and work at a pace that is appropriate to their rate of learning.

Programmed learning is another concept that falls within this category. While the great majority of these programs are available on CD-ROM, other formats still exist. These might best be typified by the ageless SRA Reading (MARI, Inc., 1-800-955-9494), available for elementary students for the past 40 years. Under this and other programmed-learning formats, students move through the instructional materials at their own pace. Specifically with SRA, students are given a placement test that determines the level at which they will start. They then work through multiple levels of booklets that contain stories, comprehension questions, and skills. For students who learn easily on their own, this format provides accelerated learning experiences that are easily monitored by students and teachers alike.

Talent Search

The talent search model has been used across the United States for decades. Through this program, students of exceptional ability are identified and made eligible for rigorous courses not usually offered in their local area. The universities that offer these programs include Duke, Northwestern, University of Denver, and Johns Hopkins. What makes these programs unique is that their primary target population is students of middle school age. Courses at some centers serve students as young as second grade.

For the most part, students are identified through high-stakes tests such as the Scholastic Aptitude Test (SAT) and the American College Test

(ACT) given at a far younger age than normal. This out-of-level testing provides a ceiling sufficient to show the true achievement of highly talented students. Unbelievably, some still earn perfect scores despite taking the tests up to 5 or 6 years early. Cutoff scores are determined for eligibility, and students scoring at that level or higher can register and participate in classes such as humanities, math, computers, and science. Residential, correspondence, online, day, and summer courses are offered at many of the sites.

Talented students participating in talent search, can take part in coursework that is challenging and above the level of content typically offered in their local schools. Students who come to campus are also given the advantage of interacting with instructors and other participants with similar interests and abilities.

Distance Learning

Opportunities for distance learning, once a promising possibility, are now a flourishing reality. Programs are available in all content areas and most grade levels throughout the world (McKinnon & Nolan, 1999). Distance learning serves many purposes for talented students. Perhaps the most significant is that students can access classes or information beyond what might be locally offered. A student with few challenging programs available can find advanced courses available through the Internet, video conferencing, videotape, courses on community access television, or other distance education methods. Of particular interest to highly talented students are advanced placement classes, dual enrollment opportunities at universities, chats with experts, demonstrations online or on video, simulations, and communication with other students of high ability.

It is hard to say what opportunities will be available in the future as this form of education is rapidly progressing. Widespread use of techniques such as virtual reality holds particular promise. Under this format, students could actually perform surgery, visit the pyramids in Egypt, speak with an image of Abraham Lincoln, fly in space, or have other amazing adventures. The opportunities for advanced study are endless. It is highly likely that distance education will become an integral part of the educational process for all students. For the talented, it promises to be a conduit to the world and its many resources.

Independent Studies

The use of the independent-study format, as the basis for program development, is extensive and particularly widespread with high-ability students (see Figures 3.3 and 3.9). In the talent development model, they can be best used as a means for organizing student investigations beyond the basic curriculum. Studying ideas at an advanced pace, in greater depth, or of interest to the student, enrich the learning environment for this population. The approach is useful for other students as well (see Box 4.1).

Even with older students, it is essential that students understand the requirements and procedures prior to the onset of the study. It may be surprising to observe that, despite unusual talent, these students may not have the skills in independent learning one might expect. It may be necessary to hold an orientation seminar to discuss guidelines for successful

---

Box 4.1   Student Guidelines for Independent Study

1. Identify a topic of sufficient depth that a comprehensive study is possible.

2. Identify a topic of sufficient focus that it has a beginning and logical end.

3. Frame your investigation in terms of questions.

4. Use many different types of resources, such as books, videos, the Internet, interviews, primary sources, and so on.

5. Plan a timeline for the study so that the time needed is within the requirements, and identify steps to take.

6. Consider multiple ways to report your findings. Select the one that best showcases the findings no later than halfway through the study.

7. Write down approximately three ways the success of the project can be determined. Use these as a culminating project activity.

8. Make frequent appointments with the study supervisor to talk about the progress of the study and talk through any issues that may arise.

9. If the project has application to real-world outcomes, make arrangements to present the findings to the appropriate parties.

---

studies. For example, a first grader will have difficulty completing a study on "Birds" as there is no logical end to the study. A study on "Birds in My Backyard" is more clearly defined and within the abilities of the student. An older student studying the impact that the Appian Way had on the Romans' ability to maintain their empire is also sufficiently focused to investigate and complete.

Products for independent studies are another aspect that may require prior discussion. Students are used to writing papers and illustrating their ideas through drawings and models. They may be less experienced at developing products such as actual scientific investigations or developing a portfolio of their sketches for evaluation by a gallery owner. The products of independent studies can be as significant to the learning experience as the actual development of the content. Process and content are both an essential part of the purpose behind offering independent-study options.

Flex Class

What is known as a flex class is an extension of the basic independent-study process. When this is used in a high school setting, a recommended top 1% of the student body is eligible as it is reserved for only the most talented students who are able to take responsibility for their learning. For in a flex class, students are given the leeway to negotiate course requirements with teachers and determine to what extent they need to be active in class. In so doing, they may have classes that they do not have to attend on a regular basis and can schedule other activities during that time. As an example, a student might have French 3, chemistry, advanced English, U.S. history, and trigonometry on their schedule. A conflict is present in that he or she also has interest in advanced biology and does not have time to do that and attend scheduled classes as well. Under the flex class notion, the student could petition teachers for a flexible-attendance pattern so that taking the sixth class would be possible. The French 3 teacher may agree to attendance only for tests. The U.S. history teacher may consider the possibility of testing out of chapters or the entire course. Attending chemistry labs only may also be a possibility. If all options open enough time for advanced biology, the student can accelerate the time spent in high school or the science content available at school.

As it is the rare student who will be prepared to use this flexible pacing structure, it is recommended that only a few students be given this status. By determining eligibility through faculty petition or recommendation (as seen in the National Honor Society procedure), the program should run smoothly as students involved will only be those with the skills and need to participate. Even with a small number of participants, the inclusion of a flex class within a program mosaic will be valuable to those students who need just this type of flexible arrangement.

Advanced Placement

Advanced placement (AP), a program available through the College Board (www.collegeboard.org/ap/), is a well-known program for high school students and is designed to offer rigorous accelerated content and the possibility of entering higher education with college credits. If their scores on the culminating AP test meet or exceed the scores deemed acceptable for this purpose by the individual universities, the colleges may choose to grant college credit or waive courses or course requirements. Talented students can earn credits sufficient to enter college as a second-semester freshman or above. About 50% of colleges offer entrance as a sophomore when the number of tests taken and the scores on those tests justify that many hours of credit. More competitive universities may even require evidence of participation in this program (or others such as International Baccalaureate or dual enrollment) for application consideration (VanTassel-Baska, 2001).

AP courses are usually taught by highly skilled high school teachers with guidance from materials available from the College Board or on their Web site feature, AP Central (apcentral.collegeboard.com/). Through this portal, teachers can access sample course descriptions, resource catalogues, reading lists, professional-development opportunities, and discussion forums. Students can find sample test questions, course and test details, registration information, and newly offered tests.

Over 8 million students have used this program and over a million take the tests each year with 62% scoring sufficiently high to receive some college credit. Thus students involved in the program can accelerate the pace of the learning at the university level as well. Among the 35 tests available in 19 content areas are Latin, physics, world history, 3D design, music theory, and English. AP is available to students worldwide.

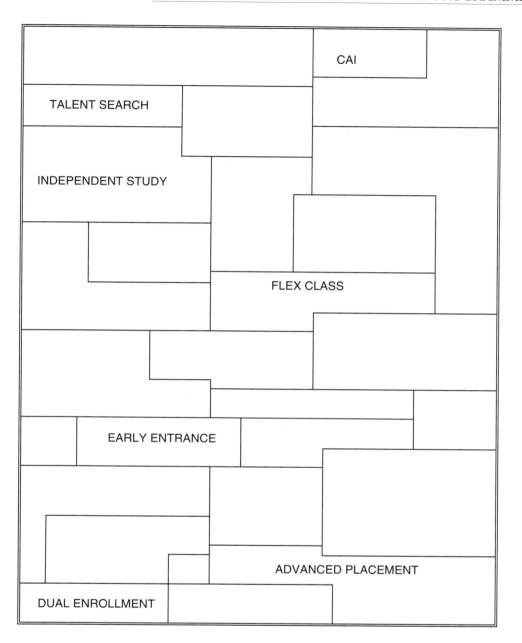

Figure 4.1
Pace Panel for
Program Mosaic

Program Mosaic for Pace

Determining which programs will be included on a pace panel, one must take a number of factors into account (see Figure 4.1). These included programs must

- Be for students at all academic levels
- Be for students across curricular content areas
- Include students of similar abilities and interests
- Be available in the community or through distance learning options

Program options can be selected from Figure 4.1, programs listed in Chapter 5, programs unique to a school district, or other programs discovered by the program planners. The pace panel, itself, should be coordinated with the panels for depth and interests so that students and program planners can access programs throughout the mosaic. This aspect, however, is essential as it contains some of the program options that will provide the rigor and challenge needed to keep talent developing through structured content, systematic review, and exposure to standards of performance considered exceptional in varying fields of study.

Depth-of-Learning Panel

Placing programs into a mosaic for the purpose of encouraging talented students to learn in depth is the second phase of program mosaic development. These programs should correspond to the student's need to understand the complexity and applicability of class content. These students often do this to a higher level, advanced from their age peers, and use this need to strengthen and advance understanding.

As stated earlier, many programs appropriate for inclusion on the depth-of-learning panel may also satisfy the defining characteristics of pace and interests. By the very nature of this category and corresponding characteristics, this is often the case. The confluence of these factors leads to the ability and desire to study the interesting content at a higher and faster level.

Exhibitions, Competitions, and Fairs

Developing projects for exhibitions, competitions, and fairs is a common way for students to engage a topic in greater depth. LEGO League, art exhibitions, and history fairs are all examples of programs that require in-depth learning for students to be successful. They are flexible in the types of learning that can take place, allowing students to interact with the experience at varying levels. In a history fair, for example, some students will explore their topics in depth, using primary sources, interviews, and other data-gathering techniques. Their commitment to the task translates into projects showing extensive knowledge of their topics and understanding of the intricacies associated with it. They become expert. Other students, at the same fair, may have projects that are adequate, but knowledge gained is obviously at a surface level. While both groups are offered the opportunity to participate in the fair, the first group has engaged the opportunity more fully.

For talent development, such programs give students the latitude to study topics in depth and select which topics they prefer for that process (Karnes & Riley, 1997). Some will choose activities in which they naturally excel. Others will select topics they wish to learn more about. Students more talented in math may choose to participate in Mental Math (www.aaamath.com/men.html), Math Olympiad (imo.math.ca/), Math League Math (www.aaamath.com/men.html), or the Canadian Mathematics Competition (camel.math.ca/CMS/Olympiads/index.html). Developing their "math sense" is a byproduct of the competitions, as strategies needed to participate successfully are part of the process. An exhibition of student sculptures, as part of an annual arts week, gives students a public showing of their work and a deadline by which projects must be completed.

Public showings and exhibition dates can motivate students to work at their highest level, using their skills of analysis, synthesis, and evaluation (Bloom, 1956).

Elective Classes

Within the school structure, elective classes are generally offered for students in Grades 1 through 12. These may include such programs as Junior Great Books (www.greatbooks.org); a before-school, foreign-language class; jazz band; seminars, Future Problem Solving (www.fpsp. org), or Philosophy for Children (www.wou. edu/las/humanities/can-non/children.htm). Students have the option of participating or not. When students choose to be part of this type of program, it can be a successful talent development opportunity. Philosophy for Children gives students strategies for thinking that are useful in other contexts. The skill application extends beyond that one program and helps develop the skills needed for in-depth learning. Foreign-language instruction does the same. It creates a new challenge in thinking because languages have their own rules that must be mastered. The flexibility in thinking required to master additional languages creates skills applicable to other areas. The more students develop such skills, the more they are able to apply them to different topical areas and cognitive processes.

Students who enjoy this type of learning are prone to become involved in many of these classes. There is danger in being overly involved, however. Judicious choices enhance learning capabilities for a lifetime. Overly committing to these activities can jeopardize success in any. High-ability students can easily fall into this trap and should be cautioned about this potential problem. Program planners must remember that offering a number of these opportunities does not result in comprehensive programming for this population. It is a valuable piece but must be coupled with options including rigorous content.

Reenactments and Simulations

Thinking about reenactments (see Chapter 5, Spotlight #41) is often set in a historical context. Students might reenact the Civil War battle at Gettysburg to better understand what happened. The expedition of Lewis and Clark is another prime event for reenactment. These activities provide students with a glimpse of what history was actually like. Sponsors hope the students, by living an approximation of the event, will develop a broader understanding of why the event occurred and its impact on the future.

Reenactments can be held as part of a class at school or as an activity of a community group. Civil War reenactments are common, as are reenactments of medieval times. Encampments are created with corresponding roles taken to support the function. Cooking, protecting, and entertaining are among the activities in which the participants engage and often specialize. Many reenactments are open to the public for interaction and observation. For some, this is a family project. Recreation vehicles are loaded, and the family travels to a weekend reenactment. Participants make clothes, gather equipment, learn new language, and adopt customs—all in the quest for authenticity.

Box 4.2   Sample Simulations

Sample Simulations and URLs

Surgery

www.vlearn3d.org/collaboration/

Space Missions

www.rice.edu/armadillo/Simulations/

3-D Anatomy

visiblep.com/

Moon Link

www.moonlink.com/

Drinking and Driving

itech1.coe.uga.edu/~lrieber/motivation/

Underwater Virtual Fishbowl

www.mos.org/whats_happening/press_releases/
991202-initiatives.html

Businesses

www.edusim.net/index2.htm

Aeronautics

www.geometry.net/science/aeronautics.php

Learning in depth is essential to the authenticity of a reenactment. It is impossible to participate without knowing the how and with what. Research is the process for finding the factors that make a reenactment authentic. For those with talent, reenactments as school or community activities can result in a successful in-depth learning experience.

Simulation is another category of activity through which talented students are well served (see Box 4.2). In simulation, participants play roles that are coordinated in such a way that the resulting experience is prototypical. They can be categorized into three types: skill, role-playing, and strategy (Ferrari, Taylor, & Vanlehn, 1999). For example, the Model United Nations simulates the roles and procedures used in the actual United Nations housed in New York City. Students assume the roles and use the systems of the real organization. They deal with political realities that an institution with varying cultures and political agendas generate, while attempting to develop worthwhile initiatives. Another form of simulation can be seen in popular computer software products that require the users to develop communities and other settings through a simulation strategy. The capacity to see how factors interrelate, generalize findings, and create and process new ideas are all abilities related to the in-depth learning that is engaged and fostered through simulation.

Original Research

Students who engage in original research are using their in-depth learning skills throughout the process. When problems are identified for study, the student has discerned some type of dissonance that requires further investigation. Framing the research questions necessitates analyzing the possible explanations for the dissonance and determining which to pursue. Complexity is reduced to simple questions. The actual research also engages in-depth learning skills as well, for students must observe and evaluate what is occurring while noting study results. Writing and disseminating these results is also an example of in-depth learning as students express their generalizations in order to convey their findings.

It should not be assumed that original research is an activity reserved for older students. Students in the early elementary grades can also participate in this process. While the studies may be basic and the results less than profound, learning the research process is a worthwhile activity. The organizing of the thoughts, discipline of observation and documents, and development of written documentation of results are all skills that are useful for students at any grade. Youngsters may explore the effect of varying levels of light on growing plants. Older students may conduct consumer research on the absorbability of different brands of paper towels, while high school students may explore the effect of carcinogens on the reproduction capabilities of mice. Serving as a lab assistant for a researcher can result in similar skill development. This role gives students the opportunity to observe and participate in research activities that may be beyond those they could generate on their own. It is likely that they will further develop their own skills as they are cognitively stretched by participating in a process that exceeds their own capabilities. Regardless of the age, research is an effective way to further develop students' capabilities to use their in-depth learning skills.

Internships, Mentorships, and Apprenticeships

Engaging students in activities that team them with community members are very successful strategies for further developing students' ability to learn in depth. Internships, mentorships, and apprenticeships are all means for doing just that. After training, community members work with students and familiarize them with the workings of their job activities. Students may be with the community volunteer for a day, a month, a semester, or for years. The extent of the contact depends on the purpose of the activity and the availability of the volunteer. Participating effectively in real-life settings forces students to draw on their skills already developed as they undertake the in-depth learning required for success.

Sites for these activities are varied and can be matched to the students' POA and availability. Among the sites at which they may be placed are a zoo, hospital, public relations firm, school central office, construction site, governmental department, plant nursery, social service agency, accounting firm, artist studio, and airport. Within the context of the experience, students can find broad learning opportunities that may extend their cognitive capabilities and career goals. Seeing what various roles the community requires can inspire students to broaden their outlook on what is expected and needed for success. New paths toward employment may emerge. Complex cognitive skills may be given authenticity when the necessity for their development becomes clear in a workplace milieu.

Clearly, students who have the opportunity to engage in a mentorship, apprenticeship, or internship may be on the threshold of a life-changing experience. The experience of bringing their skills learned in school to bear on work-related activities provides the bridge to understanding the connection of school learning to future workplace requirements. No longer do writing skills seem tangential when it is apparent that writing effective strategic plans can lead to the profitability of a business. Geography can be seen as vital to developing informational technology systems that span the world. Foreign-language requirements emerge as vital when students observe the important role bilingual ability plays in communicating with patients, clients, or coworkers. Understanding these relationships through an in-depth learning experience can have profound impact on the students who participate. Not only do they gain new information and skills but for the first time they also may get a glimpse of their future.

Program Mosaic for In-Depth Learning

Determining which programs will be included on the depth-of-learning panel, program planners should take heed of critical components needed for this type of experience (see Figure 4.2). These include

- Opportunities for students at all academic levels
- Topics across curricular-content areas
- Challenging experiences
- Complex relationships between program components
- Real-world applications for products
- Active-learning opportunities
- Community participation
- Stringent guidelines for self-evaluation and authentic assessment measures

Programs that are part of this panel should be broad in scope and challenging in content. Variety allows students to engage in activities that correspond to their need and capability for in-depth learning. These aspects are vital in making the program options substantial and are needed for the significant learning experiences such programs can create.

Interest Panel

The final mosaic panel is composed of program options that correspond to the varying interests talented students possess. These interests tend to be either unique or more similar to students of an older age. It is likely that program planners will not be able to anticipate all the interests this population will express. What becomes essential, therefore, is to use program planning as an opportunity to develop relationships that may

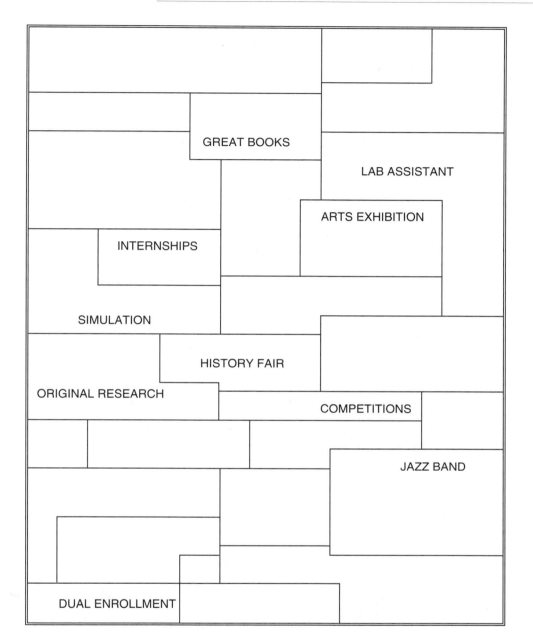

Figure 4.2
Depth-of-Learning
Panel for Program
Mosaic

lead to future programmatic liaisons. The community holds particular promise when seeking potential program partners.

Minicourses

It is not usual for talented students to be intensely interested in one topic. As with K.C. in Chapter 3, these interests can become all consuming. Minicourses are structures that can be used to increase students' knowledge of a topic or expose them to experiences that might otherwise be ignored. Some elementary schools have initiated Fun Fridays in which the last 45 minutes of each week are devoted to minicourses. Students select the courses they wish to take. The programs may have such titles as Sign

Language, Kitchen Chemistry, Measures and Weights, Making Paper, Kangaroos and You, Guitar, Spanish, and Photography with Ansel Adams. Sessions are held for a predetermined number of weeks, at which point, the options change, and students regroup. Community members, faculty, and students can comprise the talent pool from which experts are selected and programs developed.

For the talented student, the minicourses give a structure through which they can engage in activities of interest. Students interested in music might sign up for the guitar class. Students more scientifically inclined may select the courses on weights and measures or kitchen chemistry. Those interested in strategies for improving rock climbing might find a short course at the local YMCA.

Another structure for minicourses is the weekend model. In this case, schools or other organizations sponsor the courses, and the students sign up for published options. The programs typically run for approximately 10 sessions, and a cost is likely to be assigned. Such programs may take the form of camps, weekly activities, or after-school community classes. The goals of the sponsoring agency tend to determine what types of programs are offered.

Schools cannot be expected to satisfy students' interests in all areas. It is impossible, as the interests of these students vary greatly. What they can be expected to do is be aware of these interests and consider structures through which they can be addressed. Minicourses are popular as they are comparatively easy to design and implement. Community-based minicourses can provide programs that the school does not have the resources or time to mount. It is, therefore, essential, that both options be considered when program mosaics are assembled.

Field Trips

At first glance, field trips may seem like a fairly low-level activity for talented students, and it may be. The value comes when the destination captures the imagination of the participating students. You never know when an activity will do exactly that, causing planning difficulties for program planners. Field trips can be seen as diversions from the everyday schedules of school. Or they can be seen as an adventure into the previously unknown. Having a purpose for a field trip, beyond using one's allotted bus time, takes the experience from one with no expectation to one of unlimited possibility.

To include this category on a mosaic panel, it is essential that the planners of these activities pay particular attention to how such trips can bring understanding to content. A trip to a French and Indian war vintage fort extends from a quick walk around the perimeter to a treasured memory when the fort's administrators sponsor actual reenactments in which the students may participate. An aquarium visit is broadened when students are allowed to assist in the feeding of the fish. A junket to a museum is expanded in its focus when students are taken behind the scenes by the docent and witness the delicate preservation process.

Using field trips to give students a glimpse into the inner workings of a destination extends their learning and may pique their interest in topics otherwise not considered. Students of all ages can benefit as long as the trips pertain to their interests and correspond to the content they are studying at school. Drama students might take a field trip to the theater when a road production of a play is showing. Seeing a play mounted by professionals and having the chance to interview the actors, producers, musicians, and technicians after the show makes the trip far more valuable. Students may find new interests or extend those previously held through this type of engagement.

Program planners might also consider building a structure through which students can take personal field trips. Rather than always going with a school-sponsored group, the students can submit a proposal to take a personal field trip during school hours (see Table 4.2). Liability issues may prevent this option from being offered, in which case this option could become a credit-producing weekend activity.

Service Projects

Service projects (Lewis, 1996) are another structure through which students can pursue their interests. The wide variety of possibilities makes this a prime source of potential exploration. Many schools now require students to complete a service requirement prior to graduation. It may be a class with credits assigned or an individual responsibility. There is no age limitation, so students can serve the community, school, or nation anytime during their school years.

Service projects can be organized through the school or community agencies. Activities for potential service projects are unending. Students may choose to complete a project for their school, such as gathering and organizing pictures for the school's 50th anniversary celebration. Younger students may take on a service project of collecting toys for distribution to homeless children at holiday time. By looking beyond themselves, they can discover a multitude of potential projects and choose those that are of the most interest to them.

Service projects can also take the form of participation in school or community activities. Peer mediation could be termed *service*. Offering to join the school's speaker's bureau could also qualify. Writing for the local paper (see the vignette of Ben Ness, student columnist, in Chapter 3), or serving as student representative to the district's Parent Teacher Organization could also be considered service projects. Some programs even include such activities as working on the school yearbook or newspaper as a service activity.

Projects of a grander scale might also be part of the interest panel on the program mosaic. Habitat for Humanity, Students Against Drunk Driving, and Key Club are programs available throughout the country that provide exciting service possibilities. Families can sponsor service projects in their community or join service projects sponsored by community agencies or churches. Whatever the focus of the service projects, students can contribute their talents to the community while further developing their talents through application. The wide range of service options makes it easy to match student interests to actual projects. Whether formal requirements or personal need, the motivation for participation in service projects leads to further exploration of interests for those who are involved.

Extracurricular Activities

Schools sponsor a broad array of extracurricular activities that can be included in the interest panel of a program mosaic. They earn their place

Table 4.2
Personal Field Trip
Application

Name: _____

Home Room: _____

Home Phone: _____

Destination:

Purpose:

Resulting Product:

Trip Date:

Classes/Activities Missed:

Approvals/Arrangements Needed:

Student Signature: _____

Parent Signature: _____

Sponsoring Teacher Signature: _____

Liability Form on File: _____ Date: _____

Approval [＿＿＿＿]   By: _____ Date: _____

on the mosaic by offering activities that correspond to the interests students show. For the most part, these activities are mounted from the interest base that the students of a particular age typically hold. They may come in the form of clubs, sports, productions, musical groups, and leadership organizations. Students usually self select the extracurricular activities in which they have interest. Those actively involved have many opportunities to use their interests in further skill development. Being a member of the student Toastmaster's Club will extend the student's skills in public speaking while engaging in an activity that is of interest. Swimming as a member of the swim team gives students the chance to swim for their school (or club) while perfecting swimming skills and staying fit. Joining the school choir not only gives the members a chance to perform at community functions but it also leads to finer technique through the director's coaching. The products of participation often take on a far more complex nature than interest alone.

Program Mosaic for Interests

When program planners consider what programs should be included on the panel corresponding to student interests, they may wish to look beyond the school setting and include community options as well. Their evaluation of possible programs might include consideration of the following:

- Opportunities for students at all academic levels
- School, community, and nationwide options
- Possible school credit for participating students
- Skill development that can be derived from the experience
- Accessibility of programs
- Range of potential activities available
- Products that may result from participation
- Interests that students hold

Adding options to a program mosaic that are based on the interests of the students gives them the opportunity to see how they can learn from the activities they enjoy (see Figure 4.3). The divide between what they enjoy doing and the skills they need to develop is minimized. In addition, the active nature of these program options keeps learning exciting and pertinent to their lives.

Assembling the Mosaic

It is not enough to assemble the panels for pace, depth, and interests without also considering how the options fit into the whole they form when combined. To determine if that whole matches the needs of the students in a particular school, program planners might ask themselves the following questions about the potential program options they have selected. Have they included program options across all grade levels? Are the options broad in scope, including possible participation in challenging activities? Is there room for students to self-select some program options? Are the students' POAs reflected in the options contained in the mosaic? Is the community involved in sponsoring program options? Is the mosaic balanced within and between the three panels?

Figure 4.3
Interest Panel for
Program Mosaic

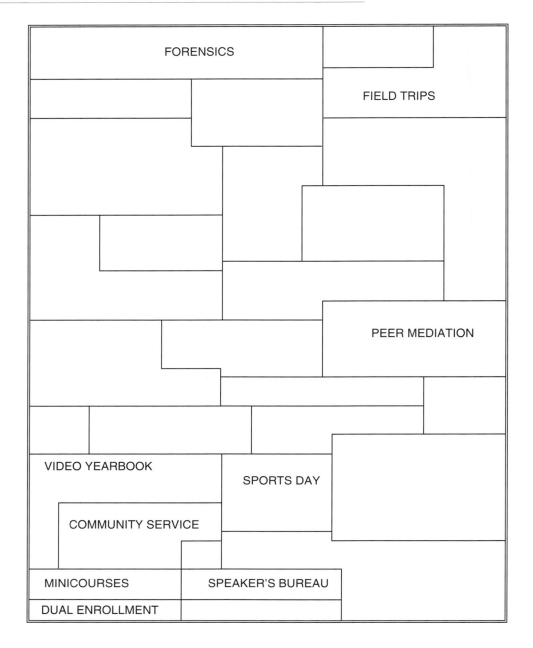

If the answers to the questions are yes, program planners can be confident that they have developed a program mosaic ready for implementation. The final judgment of adequacy will be made as students begin to use the mosaic. It is unrealistic and ill-advised to think that the mosaic is ever complete. It must be seen as an ongoing task and attended to as such. As students change, so must the mosaic. As additional opportunities are developed, they should be evaluated for possible inclusion. Student and community recommendations may also provide options to be considered. When seen as an evolving process, the mosaic can provide a resource from which POAs can be matched, giving talented students rich and challenging learning experiences (see Figure 4.4).

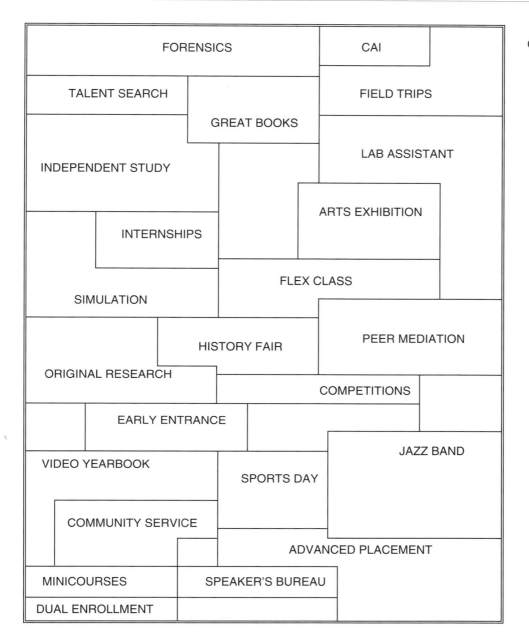

Figure 4.4
Combined Program

PARTNERS IN CHANGE ■

Mr. Spence thought it was clear that the Greenwood district could begin to mount a talent development program by acknowledging that many pertinent programs were already in place. He also found it obvious that further program development was needed. How to best accomplish this task in an environment of school reform and ever-increasing tight budgets was the problem he felt would be toughest to solve. Thinking through the issue resulted in an obvious solution. He would need to look beyond the school walls and build partnerships with the parents and the greater community. The partnership would open new possibilities for the program mosaic but also result in the relationships needed to continue to strengthen the school district in total. He decided to start with the parent organizations, parents of program students, and the members of the district's community forum. Mr. Spence felt the partnership approach to be the most likely strategy to build the mosaic needed to mount the talent development program. He decided to use the slogan "Partnerships for Change" to give the process a formal name denoting an ongoing process. He knew that members of a task force are far more likely to fully participate when they know their task is one that is serious and will result in action. The first matter the task force took into consideration was the role teachers and parents would play in order to ensure program success. While these tasks would not be easy, Mr. Spence knew they were necessary and would be a significant part of the ultimate success or failure of the initiative.

■ ROLES IN DISCOVERY AND DELIVERY OF A PROGRAM MOSAIC

It was obvious to all members of the Partners for Change task force that the district's teachers would have to buy into the talent development concept and be willing to work with the group in developing POAs and program delivery. All knew the staff was highly talented and would bring substance to the program. The ongoing professional-development program had resulted in staff members who were beginning to differentiate instruction on a broad scale and who might see this program, if framed correctly, as an extension of that training, for it surely was. Extensive thought was given to who should be asked to represent the faculty on the task force. Mr. Spence knew the GAP Group could continue in this role but would make the numbers on the task force quite large. He would consider having representatives from that group take part. It would also be necessary to include representation from each school so that there would be members from the elementary, middle school, and high school levels. Department chairs, grade level chairs, and the natural school leaders would also need to be considered as the task force must draw from as many groups as possible, giving them a voice in the planning process. His attention then turned to community members and parent leaders who could add authenticity to the project while contributing their vast talents. They, too, should be represented on the task force. In this way, they would have ownership in the evolving program and would be more likely to lead the effort toward change within their constituencies. He wrote all the names on his dry-erase board and called in Ms. Marge and Mr. Fruth for a strategy session.

It is widely accepted that program planners, initiating a talent development model, must have the support of their faculty and community in order to do so effectively. Without the critical groups behind such an effort, it will not be successful, no matter how strongly it is endorsed by the administration and board of education. Under a talent development model, teacher involvement is particularly critical as the model permeates instruction. It is embedded in all instructional decisions that are made. Talent development is a concept that drives the instruction; it is not a separate program, with separate staff, taking effect in separate classrooms, having no impact on the majority of teaching staff. Rather, it is every day, in every class, in every subject, and thus integral to the instructional practice of them all.

The influence teachers have in this model can be very empowering. Each has a role to play that is vital to the students they meet with daily. Freedman and Montgomery (1994) point out that the first teachers students have are reported to have great importance in their lives. This empowerment comes from the natural influence teachers have based on their role but also due to the vast range of factors they can influence. The roles they play in development are broad. Bloom (1985) remarked that having the right teacher at the right time was one of the critical components of talent development. Understanding this, teachers must be aware of the central role their participation plays in a strong talent development model that, hopefully, they will embrace as the manifestation of their motives for making teaching their chosen profession.

Other educational professionals also have a profound effect on the students. They, too, have key roles in the talent development process. Guidance counselors play a pivotal role in guiding students' self-awareness and career choice. School psychologists are essential in designing and implementing the assessment programs that sustain the structure of the model. Administrators are at the hub of the process as they serve as the primary curriculum leaders (Edmonds, 1979) and organizers for policy development. Even members of the local school board play a part as they approve policy and allocate funds for program development and implementation.

Guidelines for Program Planners

Researchers and experts (Barnett & Darden, 1993; Canciamilla, 1999; Feldhusen, 1996; Fulkerson, 1995; House, 2002; Kerr & Colangelo, 1988; Renzulli, 1994b; Treffinger, 1995; VanTassel-Baska, 1998) have identified numerous guidelines that seem to affect the quality of program design and implementation of talent development programs. Suggestions for program planners follow.

1. Program planners build organizational structures committed to sustained talent development (Fulkerson & Horvich, 1998; Treffinger, 1995). A program with a formal structure gives the appearance of solidity and integration in the program base of a school district. It also allows planners to assemble data needed for the informed decision making necessary for program longevity. Canciamilla (1999) suggests that program planners create a "mission" based on the goals of the program and the needs of the students. Without structure and commitment, a program can quickly collapse under the pressures associated with its implementation. As talent develops across a lifetime, the demands of talent development continue and change across the time students spend in formal schooling. Their needs will be as great as juniors in high school as they are when second graders. To this end, the program developed by educators from Lawrence Township, Indiana, under the guidance of Feldhusen (Fulkerson & Horvich, 1998), attacked this requirement by building four separate components to their talent development program. They are: Emerging Talents (kindergarten), Recognizing and Developing Talents (1-5), Developing and Nurturing Talents (6-8) and Nurturing and Refining Talents (9-12). Sustained programming and its parallel commitment to long-range program life are at the core of successful programming.

2. Program planners adopt values that support programs geared to excellence for all students. Recognizing this basic tenet of the talent development model, VanTassel-Baska (1998) states, "In the current grip of egalitarian mania, when equal outcomes—not equal opportunities—are stressed, the values associated with talent development often receive limited attention. . . . Schools must show that they value excellence" (p. 763). Educators see themselves as talent scouts (Feldhusen, 1996; Renzulli, 1994b). Through knowing the nature of talent and providing opportunities for students to display talent, teachers are in the prime position to identify students who will profit from participation in programs that focus on talent development. Their point of view strengthens the argument that talent development should be a central value that guides program development for all students.

3. Program planners engage authentic partnerships with parents and members of the community (Canciamilla, 1999; Fulkerson, 1995). Assembling partnerships with parents and community members serves many purposes. Chief among these are communication, identifying potential program sites, empowering stakeholders by giving them entrée into the decision-making structures of the program, and assembling information through which effective program decisions can be made and program features made more successful. An emphasis must be made on the word *authentic.* Parents and community members must have a full voice in the process, or they will opt out of the planning process citing a lack of influence and "better things to do."

4. Program planners sponsor ongoing professional development for all stakeholders that is comprehensive and ongoing (House, 2002). In order to have the level of knowledge and understanding necessary to develop and sustain dynamic programs that suit the varying needs of students, professional development must be continual and include those people who have influence over, or are influenced by, the talent development initiative. This includes educators, parents, community members, members of the staff that sustain school activities, and students. Topics for consideration might target information on talent, program design, evaluation strategies, process skills, organizational maintenance, and effecting change. Central to this imperative are the educators who must be knowledgeable (VanTassel-Baska, 1998). As teachers are often a student's guide, they must know their content area to the degree that they can give the talented students guidance in the direction and depth their studies can take. Being thinkers (Savage, 1998) provides talented students with models they can use to pattern their own quests for knowledge.

5. Program planners institute program goals that include lifelong learning skills as well as content mastery. Challenging content that encourages students to engage complex ideas is a fundamental goal of programs designed to develop talent. Highly talented students, however, have needs that transcend content and have impact on their courses of study and lifelong learning skills. One example relates to educational and career options. Kerr and Colangelo (1988) studied students who reached the 95th percentile or above on the ACT. When given a listing of 196 possible college majors, the selections of one half of the participants indicated only three categories for study. These were majors in engineering, health professions, and the physical sciences. Obviously, this is a narrow range. By involving students in a plethora of activities and topics, students may become more expansive when thinking about their future courses of study and career goals. Other skills that might be targeted by program planners are skills studying, communicating, researching, collaborating, and creating.

6. Program planners assemble a dynamic assessment strategy to guide decision making. In a talent development model, assessment is the basis on which program decisions are made. Assessment is used to determine student need and level of proficiency, the information on which POAs are assembled. Assessment is used to determine program effectiveness and future direction (Chalker, 1996), data that help maintain a vital program mosaic. Out-of-level testing may be needed (Barnett & Darden, 1993), as may needs assessments, authentic assessment measures, standardized testing instruments, and other tools as necessitated by the decisions to be made.

Guidelines for Educators

Teachers are central to a successful talent development model. It is not surprising, therefore, that their role has also been the topic of many articles and books. The following guidelines will assist educators in playing a central role in program success.

1. Educators establish learning environments that foster talent development and individual responsibility. Clearly, learning environment has a great impact on the ability students have to learn. To enhance talent development, the environment should be safe for individual expression (Runco & Nemiro, 1994), include students in decision making, be structured so that students take responsibility for their own behavior and learning, actively engage students in goal setting (Feldhusen, 1996), use student interests when planning program development, and put a premium on productivity (Treffinger, 1995). By so doing, educators create an environment in which students can take responsibility for their learning, explore their abilities, and display their talents.

2. Educators engage in deliberate planning (Cooper, 1998). Cooper notes that talent development must be met with deliberate planning by educators. She lists a number of aspects of planning in which educators should engage. These include a qualitatively different curriculum; high-quality, authentic experiences chosen from a continuum of service options; challenge that requires students to construct meaning; curriculum that matches the sophistication of student talent; articulated performance indices; and rigorous performance expectations. Cooper sets a high standard for educators while demonstrating the rigor for which educators of talented students must be prepared. This is only possible when comprehensive planning is in place.

3. Educators extend curricular options to talented students that are challenging and meaningful. Appropriate curricular practice has been a central topic in discussions about talent development, students, and schools. For the most part, there is consensus that curriculum should be based on national content standards established by content-specific professional organizations (Burns, 2002; Owen & Lamb, 1996); focus on content mastery (Johnson & Johnson, 1992); use specialized resources (Cooper, 1998); present students with choices from which they may choose activities (Parke, 1995); use high-powered content and processes (VanTassel-Baska, 1998) that employ probing questions (Savage, 1998); schedule time for students to think (Runco & Nemiro, 1994); and have the potential to expose talent previously undetected (Feldhusen, 1996). Educators are cautioned by Johnson & Johnson (1992) that as the quality of students' performance increases, teachers must be ready for the quantity of products to decrease.

4. Educators share their observation of talent with parents (Feldhusen, 1996) *and students involved.* The suggestion to discuss talent with the parents and students involved serves a number of purposes: Students and parents are given the chance to learn about talent; primary parties receive the information they will need for educational planning; talent is acknowledged and concomitant responsibility is established; parents and students see themselves as stakeholders in the talent development process; and additional human resources are added to the bank of talent needed to make the program successful. At times, parents and students require time to come to terms with the implications of unusual talent. This can best be accomplished when they have access to the information assembled at school.

Guidelines for Parents

Parents play a critical role in talent development from the time children are at a young age. From an extensive study of talent development, Bloom (1985) concluded that supportive families that nurtured the youngster's talent played a key role in highly developed talent during adulthood. Marek-Schroer & Schroer (1993) conclude that the early identification of talent by parents is essential to its development. This pivotal role is reflected in guidelines for parents of students with talent.

1. Parents acknowledge their children's talent and support talent development. Parents are often the first to notice unusual talent in their children. When they respond to that talent by supporting their children and providing opportunities for talent development, advancement can be even more pronounced. Parents play a key role in their children's acceptance of their ability and willingness to develop that talent. Choosing to take an active role in supporting their children's talent development gives their children an ally during the unfolding of their abilities.

2. Parents provide as many experiences and resources as possible that may help develop their children's talent. It is unlikely that schools will be able to play a comprehensive role in the talent development of any one child. It is more likely that talent will be maximized when parents and schools bring their combined resources to bear on the effort. To this end, parents should be aware of the need their children have to explore their talent and test their abilities. The shelter of one's home may be the safest place for children to do so. The home also provides a base from which children can engage in the specialized lessons and community-based experiences that can lead to advanced displays of talent. Bloom (1985) cites these factors as key when children move toward exceptional development of their talents.

3. Parents take an active role in their children's formal education (Freedman & Montgomery, 1994). All educators know that students who have parents involved in their formal education are more likely to succeed. There is no substitute for the influence parents have on the development of their children. Freedman & Montgomery cite Hester's list of seven benefits reaped through parental participation in schools (p. 41). These are increased achievement, better behavior, greater motivation, regular attendance, higher graduation rates, positive attitudes toward homework, and increased parent and community support. In terms of talent, it is likely that parents who are involved in their children's education assist in developing their talent, as children tend to respond when parents monitor and value the activities in which their children are involved. Let it not be forgotten that it is also the parents who identify, fund, provide instruments and uniforms, and drive to their children's out-of-school activities.

When parents choose to be involved in school committees, they can have an even greater voice in the talent development of their children. Parents provide context and perspective as collaborators in program development (Cavarretta, 1998). Not only can they bring their personal experiences to the program-planning process but they can also offer suggestions about community resources that can be included in the district's program mosaic.

4. Parents provide information about their children to assist program-planning efforts. It is often the parents who have the best information from which POAs can be drawn. They can trace the development of their children's abilities and are aware of the activities in which their children engage. It is the parents who have information about health, interests, friends, and study habits of their children. To the extent parents are comfortable in sharing information with the schools, they can play a critical role when students' POAs are being matched to program options. They may be asked to fund certain assessments. They may be asked to provide transportation so their children can attend a school event outside the neighborhood school. They may be asked to fund an overnight trip so the same children can take part in activities away from their home community. Parents are called on to do myriad tasks and participate in a wide variety of activities central to the development of their children. Those who choose to fully communicate with the schools increase the likelihood that their children will have comprehensive educational experiences.

Mr. Spence began the process of inviting educators, community members, and parents to join the Partners for Change task force. To his relief, his requests were greeted with enthusiastic agreement. The task force was taking shape. Mr. Spence had already done a great deal to get this project off the ground, but he knew full well that it would not be at this stage of development without the support of the GAP Group, his fellow administrators, the school board, and the many people whom he had consulted and engaged in the quest to bring a talent development model to Greenwood. He took a moment to feel pride in his accomplishment but did not

THE ULTIMATE FAMILY TRIP:

Three Families, Two Winnebagos, Grandma, and the Grand Tetons

It all started out innocently enough. My co-conspirator and twin, Cheryl, mused, "We need an adventure. Let's get the whole family together and take a trip out West. It will be great. I'm sure Mom would love to come, and it's a great age for the kids to see the rugged areas of the West. What do you think?"

"Let me think about this. You're suggesting we take three families—six adults, six kids and Mom, no less—to the mountains! You must be out of your mind. The kids alone will drive us crazy even if we do take our vans. That's thousands of miles and no Nintendo hook-up anywhere. Get real," I responded incredulously.

The idea became reality rapidly. With one phone call to the car rental agency and not one but two Winnebagos later, within a matter of minutes we were committed. The trip was on. Now the work began. As I'm the queen of the list makers, I gathered the troops and got us organized. Each child was in charge of one bag. In that bag, each packed clothes from the list I prepared. Older children selected their own clothes. "If you don't pack it, you won't have it," I said.

My sister Mary is also a planner, and she took on the task of planning the trip. She provided each child with a map and tour book. And she asked the children to create a list of where they wanted to go and what they wanted to see. She then compiled the itinerary that took us through 15 states in 15 days.

Cheryl, you remember her, the genius who came up with this idea, is a health and physical education teacher. So, as usual, she was in charge of the entertainment. When departure day came, no one was surprised as the bikes, Frisbees, baseballs, and roller blades were piled in and on top of the vehicles.

The trip itself was glorious. Everyone agreed that the Grand Tetons was the favorite stop. Whitewater rafting, hiking, wild flower identification, bison spotting, and country music made for a fabulous immersion in western life. The kids endured my reading passages from the tour books about the historic significance of it all. Each wrote fact-packed "What I did on my summer vacation" essays the first week back at school, drawn from the journals each kept while traveling. I remain amazed at the vivid memories each has of Gramma by the campfire telling stories; Aunt Cheryl mountain biking in Jackson Hole, Wyoming; the chilliness of the mountain waters; the spicy beans from the roadside stand in New Mexico; Old Faithful; four Presidents looking down on them from Mt. Rushmore; and the Corn Palace in Mitchell, South Dakota, actually decorated with corn.

It took a lot of planning, effort, persuasion, engineering, and driving, but this much I know. Our family has a treasure to remember, and our children have a lifetime of memories. For me, I think of the love we share, the knowledge of the West gained first hand, and the fellowship of family. As a former teacher, I know the time was also valuable for the observation, writing, history, science, research, listening, sense of fair play, and reading skills the children used along the way. This was summertime well spent and lovingly relived at the Thanksgiving table.

dwell on the feeling. The planning work had paid off in the enthusiasm that the task force members exhibited for the program development yet to be done. He reminded himself not to get ahead of the process. It was going to take years in development and years in maintenance to meet the needs of the very talented Greenwood students and their brothers and sisters yet to come.

CONCLUSION ■

Hidden programs become inspired programming when all stakeholders take part in the development and implementation of program mosaics. The matching of students' POAs to programming options drawn from the program mosaic is most effective when representatives of all stakeholders participate. Through the collaborative process, the talents of the community, school, and home can merge into vital programming for students. Community members and agencies, school personnel, and families all have a role to play. The more fully they play that role and contribute to the development of their children, the more fully the talent development efforts will be actualized.

POINTS TO PONDER ■

- Program mosaics provide a structure through which student POAs can be matched to programming options.
- Program mosaics include panels that correspond to the defining characteristics of talented students. These are pace, depth of learning, and interests.
- There are many programs that correspond to each panel of the mosaic.
- Program planners must select programming options that best suit the various needs of the students with which they work.
- When stakeholders merge and are directed by the goal of appropriate programming for all students, comprehensive programs emerge.
- Program planners, teachers, and parents all have an integral role to play when developing programs for talent development.

5

Sixty-Five Programs That Develop Talent

Programs that include characteristics responsive to the learning needs of talented students abound in schools, communities, and homes. Many paradigms have been proposed for evaluating the extent to which an individual program will make this connection. For the purpose of this chapter, programs have been included based on seven factors. These are the extent to which they:

1. Relate to the pace and depth of learning and the interests talented student may hold

2. Represent a variety of programs at each LoS model level (Treffinger, 1998)

3. Reflect the program standards published by the National Association for Gifted Children (1998) (see Resource A) and by The Association for Gifted (1989) (see Resource B) (see also Resource C)

4. Provide a balance of examples at the elementary, middle school, junior high school, and high school levels

5. Are sponsored by schools, community, and home

6. Have been successfully implemented

7. Display at least one telltale sign of a hidden program (see Chapter 3)

The reader should be cautioned that these are representative programs that are included as examples and as a starting point to which additional programs can be added locally. They do not represent a program; they are potential pieces of a program mosaic. To mount a full-service program that corresponds to the differing Profiles of Ability displayed in any group of students, a variety of options will be needed that supply challenge and extended-learning opportunities.

By thinking creatively, being willing to take risks, communicating with colleagues and community members, and listening to the students, you will find that exciting program options will emerge.

⧼1⧽ Spotlight On: 4-H

Description. 4-H is a program of the U.S. Department of Education geared to students ages 5 to 19. It has been in existence for over 100 years. All 50 states and most counties report programs that are administered by their local Cooperative Extension Service. Approximately 7 million students throughout the United States and some other countries are actively involved in programs organized under 4-H. The 4-H pledge describes the meaning of the title: "I pledge my **H**ead to clearer thinking, my **H**eart to greater loyalty, my **H**ands to larger service, and my **H**ealth to better living for my club, my community, my country and my world." In most cases, there are no dues, as many 4-H programs are locally sponsored or funded in full from other than participant funds. Students typically do pay for their projects and activities. The projects are one of the primary activities that students engage in through 4-H. Projects are selected by the participants and can be a year in development. These in-depth activities can focus on a number of different project areas. The most familiar include animal care, sewing, baking, and craft projects. However, 4-H projects extend much further. Some 4-H chapters also sponsor projects on health, wellness and safety, workforce development, computer technology, environment, and community development. Many 4-H participants receive payment for their projects when local businesses buy their projects as a means of supporting the program. It may be surprising to learn that 4-H programs, often associated with rural settings, can be found in urban and suburban areas.

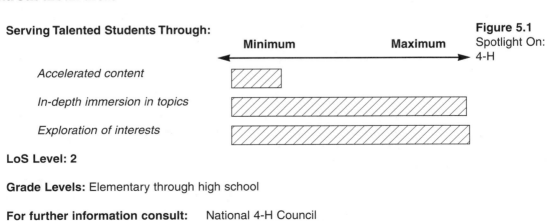

Serving Talented Students Through:

	Minimum	Maximum
Accelerated content		
In-depth immersion in topics		
Exploration of interests		

Figure 5.1
Spotlight On: 4-H

LoS Level: 2

Grade Levels: Elementary through high school

For further information consult: National 4-H Council
7100 Connecticut Avenue
Chevy Chase, MD 20815
1-301-961-2800
fourthcouncil.edu/

Spotlight On: Academic Competitions

Description. There are many types of academic competitions in which students can engage. Some are sponsored locally. Others are sponsored on the state, national, and international level. Competitions are offered in a wide range of curricular and extracurricular areas. Spelling bees, Odyssey of the Mind, Future Problem Solving, and the Academic Decathlon are examples that are found in numerous school districts. However, there are hundreds of others as compiled by Tallent-Runnels and Candler-Lotven (Corwin, 1996). For those who see advantage in competition, students can gain knowledge of their topics, confidence, team-building skills, learning strategies, and public-presentation skills through participation. See Table 5.1 for a representative sample.

Table 5.1
Sample Academic
Competitions

Competition	URL
H. S. Communications Contest	www.nfpw.org
Stock Market Game	www.smg2000.org
USA Computing Olympiad	www.usaco.org/
Very Special Young Playwrights	wata.org
Word Masters	wordmasterschallenge.com/
Young Astronaut's Program	www.yac.org

Figure 5.2
Spotlight On:
Academic
Competitions

Serving Talented Students Through:

LoS Level: 3

Grade Levels: Elementary through high school

For further information consult: M. K. Tallent-Runnels & A. C. Candler-Lotven. (1995). *Academic Competitions for Gifted Students: A Resource Book for Teachers and Parents.* Thousand Oaks, CA: Corwin.

    Spotlight On: Accelerated Readers

Description. Accelerated Readers and Accelerated Math are computer-based programs, available through Renaissance Learning (www.renlearn.com), that coordinate skill development with a self-paced evaluation structure. Students work through preselected books or math skills and use a software program of quizzes to show mastery of content. Accelerated Readers are widely used for students of all age groups and contains well-known titles as well as challenging titles. Sample titles for quizzes include the following:

- *Babbitt* by Sinclair Lewis
- *Caddie Woodlawn* by Carol Ryrie Brink
- *Clifford's First Christmas* by Norman Bridwell
- *Dear Mr. Henshaw* by Beverly Cleary
- *The Indian in the Cupboard* by Lynne Reid Banks
- *Jackie Robinson* by Richard Scott
- *Of Mice and Men* by John Steinbeck

Accelerated Math contains a wide variety of skills appropriate for students in preschool through high school. Advanced math skills, such as calculus, probability and statistics, and physics are included and can be used for students at any age level who have that level of knowledge. Samples of fourth-grade skills include

Topic 1. Whole numbers: add and subtract

Topic 2. Whole numbers: multiply and divide

Topic 3. Fractions

Topic 4. Decimals

Topic 5. Measurement, time, and temperature

Topic 6. Perimeter, area, and volume

Topic 7. Graphs, probability, and statistics

Depending on the software library selected, reports can be generated for use by teachers at student conferences, students for self-evaluation and planning, or parents for information on their children's progress in math or reading. Students can be placed at a level corresponding to their skill levels through placement tests.

Serving Talented Students Through:

	Minimum	Maximum
Accelerated content	/////////////////////////	
In-depth immersion in topics	/////////	
Exploration of interests	/////////	

Figure 5.3
Spotlight On:
Accelerated Readers

LoS Level: 1

Grade Levels: Preschool through high school

For further information consult: www.renlearn.com

 Spotlight On: Archaeological Digs

Description. Archeological digs are among those activities in which you can make it as simple as digging in the back yard or as complex as contributing to the excavation of an actual archeological site. Sites can be

contrived by constructing a site in which artifacts are placed, accessed through cyberspace, or visited in your surrounding area. There are opportunities, when using the Internet, where students can follow actual digs by reading the online journals being kept by the archeologists and viewing artifacts on Web sites. Teachers and parents can select items for backyard digs through which students reconstruct the civilization they represent. Students of all ages can work as archeologists by participating in actual digs of civilizations, animal artifacts, or unidentifiable pieces. The content and complexity of the dig can vary based on student age, knowledge of other civilizations and artifacts, and interest in the process or content. Outcomes for students are many. Among the most prominent is the opportunity to engage in metacognitive tasks, authentic activities and contexts, apprenticeship learning, student-directed goals, and primary-source data (Brown, Chou, Goldberg, & Moretti, 1991). Publications have also become available that can be used to develop, follow, or participate in archaeological digs. Foremost in this category are: *Archaeology* (www.archaeology.org) and *Dig Magazine* (www.digmagazine.com). Programs are also available through which students and families can participate in archaeological digs throughout the world.

Figure 5.4
Spotlight On:
Archaeological Digs

	Minimum	Maximum
Accelerated content		
In-depth immersion in topics		
Exploration of interest		

LoS Level: 1

Grade Levels: Elementary through high school

For further information consult: Archaeological Institute of America at: www.archaeology.org/online/features/pompeii/index.html

   Spotlight On: Ask an Engineer

Description. Ask an Engineer is a Web site, sponsored by the Pittsburgh (PA) Section of the Society of Women Engineers, at which students can ask questions related to all facets of engineering. The service is directed toward students, teachers, and parents seeking information about what engineers do, professional life, and the principles of engineering. Women in engineering is another topic that students may pursue. Questions that students ask are posted on the Web site with their corresponding answers. This is a place for students, not professional engineers, to interact with practicing female engineers. At the Web site, students can find answers to questions such as

- How did you become interested in your work?
- What types of engineering are more math based and less physics based?

- How do engineers use the concept of thermal expansion in their work?
- What effect will the introduction of antifreeze (propylene or ethylene) in a quantity not to exceed 1 gallon have on a septic system tank and field?

These services are particularly well suited to students who are making career plans, seek technical information, and are researching women in the workplace. A link is provided to How Stuff Works (www.howstuffworks.com).

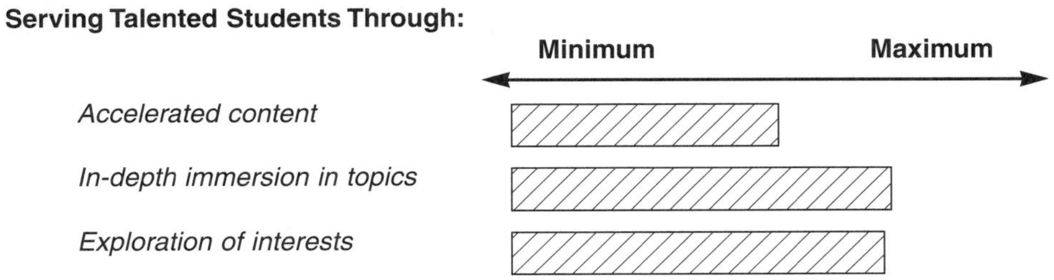

Serving Talented Students Through:

Figure 5.5
Spotlight On:
Ask an Engineer

LoS Level: 1

Grade Levels: Middle to high school

For further information consult: www.expage.com/page/askanengineer

☆6☆   Spotlight On: Block Scheduling

Description. Block scheduling is a format through which secondary school schedules are constructed to include four 90-minute periods per day. Content is delivered through intense semester-long classes. An entire year of subject matter is compressed into one semester. Students can take up to eight subjects in an academic year. (A typical high school schedule includes seven classes taken across the academic year.) With block scheduling, then, students can take an additional course and have a greater amount of sustained time to study the subject area. This may allow for more in-depth study of the subjects presented in the curriculum. It also provides a format through which students can take an additional course during the academic year. This is particularly helpful for talented students who may wish to take higher level or enrichment classes and opportunities that are not easily contained within typical schedules that do not allow enough hours in the school day. Some districts use a seminar class as one of the periods that allows students to work on independent studies, apprenticeships, and mentorships. The implementation of block scheduling has been very controversial. It has been studied throughout the United States with varying conclusions being reached. Proponents cite advantages for teachers including more time for planning and classes; flexibility in the day; and fewer students per term (www sciences.drexel.edu/block/ profpaper/smith.html). See Table 5.2 for a sample schedule.

Table 5.2
Sample Block
Schedule

	Monday	Tuesday	Wednesday	Thursday	Friday
7:35-9:00	1	2	1	2	1
9:09-10:34	3	Enrichment	3	Enrichment	3
10:43-12:38	5	4	5	4	5

Figure 5.6
Spotlight On:
Block Scheduling

Serving Talented Students Through:

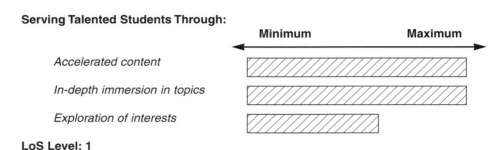

Accelerated content

In-depth immersion in topics

Exploration of interests

LoS Level: 1

Grade Levels: High school

For further information consult: P. Robbins, G. Gregory, & L. Herndon. (2000). *Thinking Inside the Block Schedule: Strategies for Teaching in Extended Periods of Time.* Thousand Oaks, CA: Corwin.

     Spotlight On: Co-Teaching

Description. Co-teaching is a model for instructional delivery. More typically found in special education and general education partnerships, co-teaching is also a process through which general education teachers can cooperate in bringing content to their students in a way that will better serve the needs of their students. By using this model, students have the benefit of two teachers' knowledge, possible varying teaching styles, more independent instruction, and team planning. There are many formats for co-teaching (Hughes & Murawski, 2001). Among these are one class two teachers, two classes two teachers, one class one teaching/one assisting, and one class one teaching large group/one teaching small group. By using varying configurations, instruction can be more personalized for students as teachers can address individual needs simultaneous to instruction. During lecture time, the collaborating teacher can answer individual question, translate concepts, and embellish or extend the content. In this way, students are in the enviable position of differentiated instruction within the context of whole group or small group instruction. Instruction and assignments gain flexibility otherwise more difficult to accomplish. To work effectively, teachers require compatible planning times.

Serving Talented Students Through:

Minimum   Maximum

Accelerated content

In-depth immersion in topics

Exploration of interests

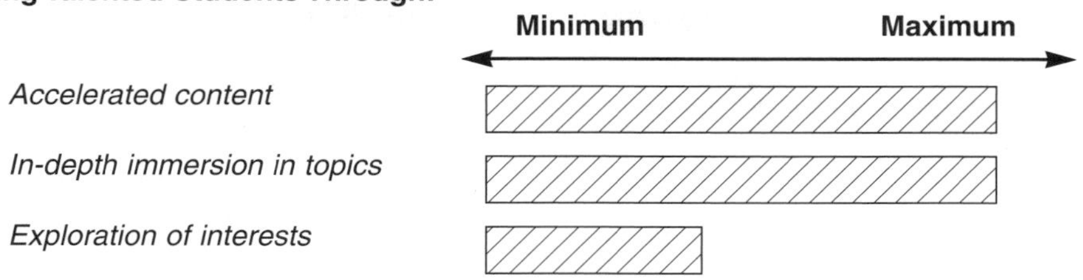

Figure 5.7
Spotlight On:
Co-Teaching

LoS Level: NA

Grade Levels: Elementary to high school

For further information consult: C. E. Hughes & W. A. Murawski. (2001). Lessons From Another Field: Applying Co-Teaching Strategies to Gifted Education. *Gifted Child Quarterly, 45*(3), 195-204.

8. Spotlight On: Community Service

Description. Community service is a concept that more and more schools are beginning to consider as part of their curricular package. In its simplest form, community service is a program through which students and families are engaged in activities that benefit their community. These might be local in focus, such as painting the house of an elderly person or reclaiming the bank of a polluted stream. Caroling at a home for the aged, recycling, or collecting food for the local food bank might also be considered. There are also community service programs that are aligned with projects of larger scope, such as Habitat for Humanity (www.habitat.org/) and UNICEF (www.unicef.org/). Service learning is another strategy that can be used that is closely tied to community service. The two concepts differ in that community learning aligns service with a school curriculum. Students are also encouraged to engage in reflective practice as part of the activity. Benefits of this type of activity include: community awareness, increased self-esteem, social responsibility, higher-level thinking skills, content skills, and character development (Howard, 1993). Additional community service projects that include the broader world community can be seen in the Table 5.3.

Serving Talented Students Through:

Minimum   Maximum

Accelerated content

In-depth immersion in topics

Exploration of interests

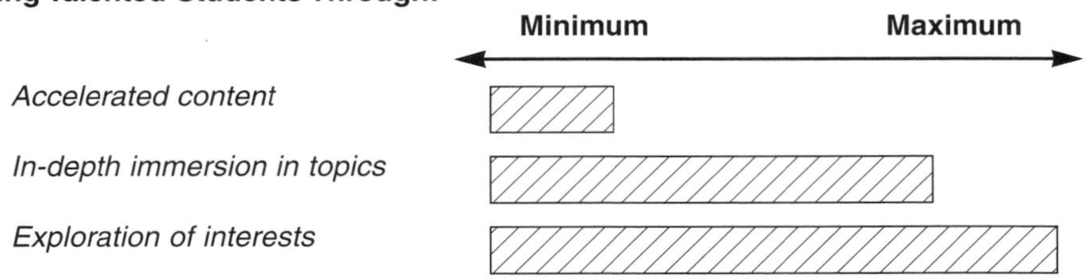

Figure 5.8
Spotlight On:
Community Service

LoS Level: 1

Grade Levels: Elementary through high school

For further information consult: L. Duper. (1996). *160 Ways to Help the World: Community Service Projects for Young People.* New York: Facts on File.

Table 5.3
Sample Community
Service Web Sites

Program	URL
Students for Students International	www.s4si.org
Urban Programs Resource Network	www.urbanext.uiuc.edu
Youth Venture	www.youthventure.org
World Wise Schools	www.peacecorps.gov/wws/service/ whatservice.html

 Spotlight On: Computer Techs

Description. Most schools have a number of activities available for students to contribute their expertise to different facets of the school community. Among these are the students who serve as computer techs. These students assist other members of the community on matters pertaining to technology, and computers in particular. They are available to set up systems, do minor maintenance, serve as mentors to other students and faculty, work on technology committees, and advise computer clubs. By so doing, these students have the opportunity to develop skills and contribute to their school. Through such opportunities, students are in the position to build self-esteem, gain technical expertise, contribute to their school, and be seen as an expert. Other similar opportunities are also available. These might include: library aides, teacher's aides, lab assistants, and medics. One is cautioned not to assign gender to these positions as both males and females are involved in the corresponding careers of each. The training needed to effectively serve in these positions is ongoing. In most of these fields, knowledge is rapidly expanding and students must work in order to be up-to-date in the requirements of the area. Computer techs must keep abreast of the technology field that is constantly changing in equipment, software, the Internet, and programming. Teaching assistants must gain the skills needed to work within inclusive classrooms. Medics must be aware of the ever-changing policies that relate to such topics as blood-borne pathogens, medications, and first aid. These positions are often an afterthought when looking for programs to develop student abilities. In fact, they are among the most effective ways to give students a glimpse of the careers to which their interests lead.

Figure 5.9
Spotlight On:
Computer Techs

Serving Talented Students Through:

Minimum   Maximum

Accelerated content

In-depth immersion in topics

Exploration of interests

LoS Level: 1

Grade Levels: Elementary through high school

For further information consult: Your local school's policy manual

Spotlight On: Debate and Forensics

Description. Debate and Forensics is a program that can be implemented at any level of educational training. Opportunities to participate in debate are typically found at the high school or middle school levels. However, elementary students can also be involved in the debate process successfully. Students engaged in this type of program may have the opportunity to develop a number of skills that will serve them well throughout their lives. Debaters learn while engaging in the process to think critically about issues, research topics, organize their thoughts in a logical manner, present their ideas in a persuasive manner, speak confidently in front of others, work effectively with team members, and function within a competitive context. The most typical way in which debate is organized involves these steps:

1. A team of students is assembled.

2. A debate league is identified.

3. Topics for debate are determined.

4. Students research topic issue.

5. Arguments are developed on both sides of the issue.

6. Students attend debate.

7. Arguments are assigned to teams (pro versus con).

8. Debate is conducted.

9. Debate is scored.

10. Scores are released.

Students at upper levels are most likely to follow this formal format. Debate leagues are common at the high school and middle school levels. Younger students are equally well served by learning to research topics, evaluate information assembled, develop arguments, work in teams, and present arguments in a succinct and persuasive manner. Absent of leagues, classroom debate is also a strong curricular choice.

Serving Talented Students Through:

	Minimum	Maximum
Accelerated content	▨	
In-depth immersion in topics	▨▨▨▨▨▨▨▨▨	
Exploration of interests	▨▨▨▨▨	

Figure 5.10
Spotlight On: Debate and Forensics

LoS Level: 3

Grade Levels: Elementary through high school

For further information consult: Yahoo site for high school debate and forensics: dir.yahoo.com/SocialScience/Communications/Forensics/Debate/HighSchool

Spotlight On: Distance Learning

Description. Distance learning has become common in school districts throughout the world. The increase in home schooling, online resources, technology in the schools, and concern that students be engaged in programs at their achievement level have raised the interest in this type of learning. Surprisingly, even elementary students are engaged in distance learning. Distance learning provides the structure through which students can take advanced-placement courses, attend a virtual high school, accelerate their time in high school, increase their skills in technological areas, work collaboratively with students throughout the world, follow the events such as the Iditarod online, take more classes than their school schedule will allow, work on a high school diploma, or participate in classes (such as foreign languages and advanced mathematics) not offered in the local school. Where distance learning used to be the last option for gaining access to needed classes, it is now seen as a favored experience in and of itself. All students need to have distance-learning skills as more and current information is often found in online formats. Rural and urban schools are particularly well served through the distance-learning format. Students can use the Internet, satellite television, videotape, and CD-ROM as formats for gaining entrance into the distance learning systems. Students who select the distance learning model must have skills in using the technology required, writing, the necessary hardware, self-discipline, and the time to be engaged in the classes for many hours per day.

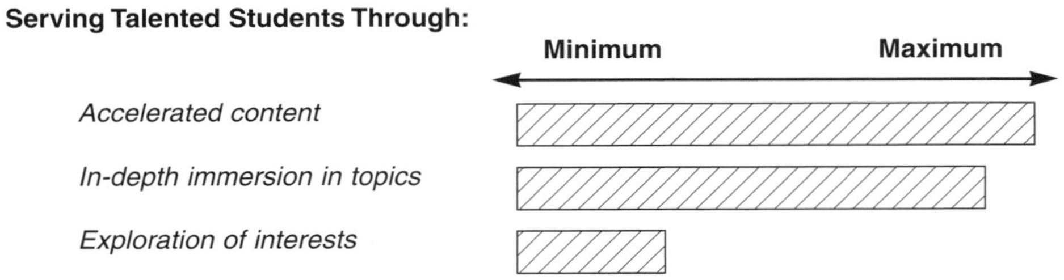

Figure 5.11
Spotlight On:
Distance Learning

Serving Talented Students Through:

	Minimum	Maximum
Accelerated content		
In-depth immersion in topics		
Exploration of interests		

LoS Level: 2

Grade Levels: Elementary through high school

For further information consult: Peterson's Guides (Ed.). (2002). *Peterson's Guide to Distance Learning Programs.* Trenton, NJ: Thompson Learning.

Spotlight On: Dress-Up Box

Description. Every home, preschool, and kindergarten has a dress up box. What may be missing is an understanding of the benefits the creative play that results from children using this box elicits. With a dress-up box, children have the opportunity to become anyone they wish. A fireman, nurse, mother, princess, truck driver, father, ballerina, teacher, or viking is just a hat away. By including exotic and mundane items in the box, children can develop intricate play as they try out the roles their clothing suggests. Play is the work of childhood. It is through play that children learn to be acclimated to their surroundings and life. Children learn to work together, use language to express themselves, safely engage in the interactions of life, and develop their creativity. It is not likely that you will find a dress-up box or housekeeping area in classrooms above the kindergarten level. However, families that keep a dress up box beyond that age, find that children continue to use its entrée to fantasy for many more years. Surprisingly, children ages 10 to 12 may still be dipping into the box to find the props needed to develop a character to be used in their play. The little ones may be students while the older child may be the teacher. The older child may be the superhero while the younger children are the focus of the rescue. Props retrieved from the dress up box bring reality to fantasy and increase the reality the children feel in their play. Parents should be encouraged to keep the dress up box available beyond the years of childhood. Even though it is a source of mess in the play area, they should be assured that the benefit to their children transcends the irritation with a basement in which crowns, stoles, swords, and high heels are strewn around the floor.

Serving Talented Students Through:

	Minimum	Maximum
Accelerated content		
In-depth immersion in topics		
Exploration of interests		

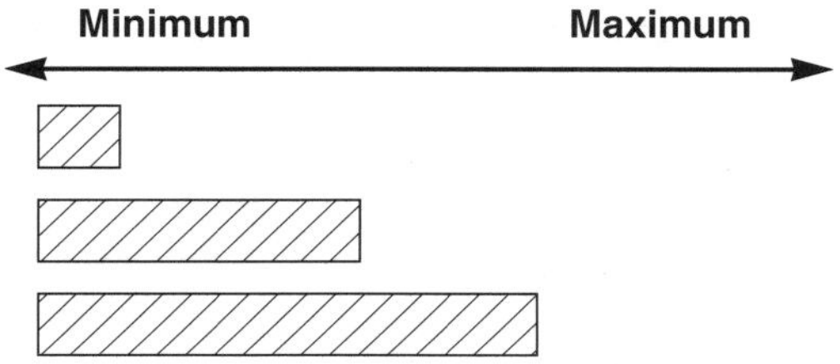

LoS Level: 1

Grade Levels: Elementary

Figure 5.12
Spotlight On:
Dress-Up Box

For further information consult: J. P. Isenberg & M. R. Jalongo. (2001). *Creative Expression and Play in Early Childhood* (3rd ed.). Upper Saddle River, NJ: Prentice Hall.

⌘13⌘ Spotlight On: Dual-Language Instruction

Description. Dual-language instruction can come in many forms. For some, it is within the context of a language immersion class in which students receive instruction in more than one language in order to teach students a second language. Students may be taught in Spanish in the morning and English in the afternoon. Often this will be found in the magnet school context. Dual language can also be structured as a course in which students meet regularly and learn a foreign language, such as French, within the elective course. Again, the purpose is to give students the basics they need to speak in a second language. A third manner in which dual language instruction is structured is through what is called English as a new language (ENL), formally known as bilingual education or biliterate education. With ENL, learning English, in order to become acclimated to a new country, is the primary goal of the class. The benefits of this type of instruction are obvious (Thomas & Collier, 1997). As the country becomes more global in its outlook, fluency in multiple languages is growing in its necessity. Business, education, travel, simple communication are all finding a greater need for alternative languages. This challenging cognitive task also builds cognitive ability. It is appropriate for instruction at the earliest of grades as children's brains are physiologically ready to accept this type of instruction. At the point that the alternative language is fully assimilated, students will actually think in the second language. Students report that they think in the language in which a question is asked. While foreign language instruction has been an enrichment option in the past, it is now a necessity of life.

Figure 5.13
Spotlight On:
Dual-Language
Instruction

Serving Talented Students Through:

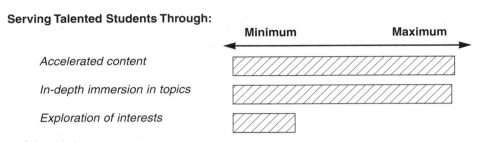

Accelerated content

In-depth immersion in topics

Exploration of interests

LoS Level: 2

Grade Levels: Elementary through high school

For further information consult: H. L. Smith. (2000, April 1). *Dual-Language Programs: Lessons From Two Schools.* Retrieved from www.scottforesman.com/ educators/letters/bilingual/smith.html
Also see www.cal.org/ericcll (ERIC Clearninghouse on Language and Linguistics) and www.ncbe.gwu.edu/ncbepubs/directions/14.pdf (National Clearinghouse for Bilingual Education).

 Spotlight On: E-Pals

Description. E-Pals, an international program with over 4 million participants in 191 countries, is used by Stanford and Siders (2001) in their study on E-Pal writing. They conducted a study in which middle-school students were paired with university teacher-education candidates as pen pals. Half of the students used the typical writing method while the other half corresponded through e-mail. Twice a week for 20 minutes a session, students (pairing students with and without disabilities) worked on pen pal composition. Results of the study showed that the group who used e-mail showed improvement for each participant. The other group did not register the same level of improvement. Programs such as E-Pals motivate both skilled and challenged writing students. The immediate feedback, novelty of writing online, available tools (such as spell and grammar check), and expectation of response from the E-Pal naturally motivates the participants. Stanford and Siders offer these suggestions when designing such a program: pair students with an E-Pal that has strong writing skills, as they will serve as a model; employ corresponding E-Pals to give feedback on writing skills to their correspondents; and make sure that all participants have the proper skills, technology, and accessibility prior to the start of the project. At the E-Pals Web site (www.epals.com), further suggestions can be found. Also, the Web site displays instructions in eight languages (including Chinese, Arabic, Spanish, and German), gives sample correspondence, lists communication tools, and sponsors E-Pal events.

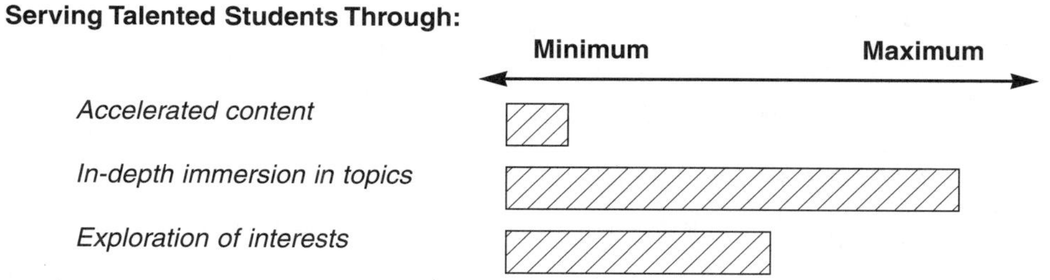

Serving Talented Students Through:

Figure 5.14
Spotlight On:
E-Pals

Minimum   Maximum

Accelerated content

In-depth immersion in topics

Exploration of interests

LoS Level: 1

Grade Levels: Elementary

For further information consult:
353 Dalhousie Street, 3rd Floor
Ottawa, Ontario
Canada K1N 7G1

E-Pals Classroom Exchange
70 Soundview Drive
Easton, Connecticut
USA 06612
1-800-613-562-9847
Toll free: 1-888-770-3333
Fax: 1-613-562-4768

⁂15⁂   Spotlight On: Family Excursions

Description. Can the weekend family excursion result in talent development? Absolutely. When children and youth accompany their families to destinations near or far from home, the experience can result in significant development of talent. Take, for example, a family excursion to the Mammoth Cave National Park in south central Kentucky. Almost two million people visit Mammoth Cave each year and explore the Park, which covers approximately 53,000 acres. Those who visit the caves can learn about the geography of the area, history of the caves, science of stalactite and stalagmite generation, spelunking, and the career of a forest ranger. It is this type of family event that can shape the participants' interests and career aspirations. On a trip to the Art Institute of Chicago, armor, ceramics, photographs, Chagall's stained glass windows, special events (such as the paintings of Van Gogh and Gauguin), and the extensive permanent collections are all on display. A day can easily be filled with the exploration of the magnificent collections of the museum. Again, the resulting effects are many. History, politics, techniques of art, careers as curators, and art appreciation are all content outcomes that are easily obtained. While in Chicago, it is only steps to the Natural History Museum (in which Sue, the largest reassembled dinosaur, is on display), Shedd Aquarium, Adler Planetarium and Astronomy Museum, and Children's Museum. A day's excursion can result in a significant exposure to the world's wonders. The excursion does not need to be as grand a junket as a trip to Chicago's Miracle Mile. The grocery store, church, mechanic's garage, beauty salon, fast food restaurant, or boutique can also have surprising impact when children are engaged in the many learning opportunities that each presents to the family on the go.

Figure 5.15
Spotlight On:
Family Excursions

Serving Talented Students Through:

	Minimum	Maximum
Accelerated content	▨	
In-depth immersion in topics	▨▨	
Exploration of interests	▨▨▨▨▨▨▨▨▨▨	

LoS Level: 1

Grade Levels: Elementary through high school

For further information consult: C. Loomis & C. Paul. (2001). *Fodor's Family Adventures: More than 700 Great Trips for You and Your Kids of All Ages.* New York: Fodor's Travel Publications.

 Spotlight On: Family Investigations

Description. Family investigations are projects, undertaken by the family, that study a problem or question in depth. These investigations may be sponsored by the school or proposed by a family member. A school may sponsor a trip to a museum that is structured through a treasure hunt developed by school or museum personnel. The family works together to complete the treasure hunt by finding different pieces of information or artifacts throughout the museum's collection. Family science projects displayed at a family science fair is another of endless possibilities. A member of a family may also propose a family investigation. Similar to the school-sponsored format, a question can be posed for the family to answer. The investigation may take the family a trip to a historical spot. A kitchen biology project may emerge or travels through the World Wide Web may result. Such investigations have the benefit of bringing the power of "family-think" to a question as individual questions are answered. Families are encouraged to focus on questions or problems offered by any family member without placing value on some being more worthy than others. Ideas posed by the youngest family members should be seen as equally important as those offered by older family members. A combination can result in the type of challenge that develops the skills needed for successful investigation for family members of all ages.

Figure 5.16
Spotlight On:
Family Investigations

Serving Talented Students Through:

	Minimum	Maximum
Accelerated content	▨▨▨	
In-depth immersion in topics	▨▨▨▨▨	
Exploration of interests	▨▨▨▨▨	

LoS Level: 1

Grade Levels: Preschool to high school

For further information consult: M. G. Hickey. (1998). *Bringing History Home: Local and Family History Projects Grades K-6.* Boston: Allyn & Bacon.
P. Murphy, E. Klages, & L. Shore. (1996). *The Science Explorer: Family Experiments From the World's Favorite Hands-on Science Museum.* New York: Henry Holt.

Spotlight On: Field Trips

Description. Field trips are one of the most popular activities for students in elementary through the high school grades. Even trips to the local pickle factory can bring great excitement to the attending class. Typically, teachers tie field trips to the curriculum being taught. They can range from hiking the Appalachian Trail to a day at the downtown Lincoln Museum. Depending on the age of the students and the curriculum being taught, teachers design field trips in order to bring their curricular goals to life. A student visiting the Lincoln museum has the opportunity to listen to the Lincoln-Douglas debate; take home a Lincoln penny; locate the many homes he lived in throughout Kentucky, Indiana, and Illinois; and become familiar with Lincoln's life through the living timeline. There are times when the desired field trip is not immediately accessible or funds are not available for a trip. Cyber trips are now available online. Through e-trips, classes can visit the White House (www.whitehouse.gov/kids/), the architecture of ancient Egypt (www.uen.org/utahlink/tours/fieldtrips2.htm), or microscopic organisms at a microbial zoo (www.accessexcellence.org/RC/virtual.html). Such adventures have many positive outcomes. Among these are immersions in rich learning environments, interactions with primary resources, socializing with peers, real-world connections with curricular goals, exploration of interests, and in-depth investigations. When students look back on their time in school, it is often the field trips that they remember. On-site learning is powerful and has lasting impact on its participants. It is not unusual for a student to tie interest in a topic back to an earlier class field trip. While they are a challenge for teachers and chaperones, the impact on students is well worth the effort.

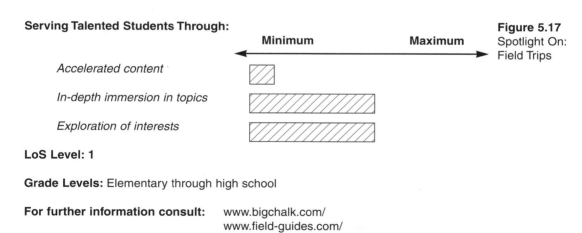

Figure 5.17
Spotlight On:
Field Trips

LoS Level: 1

Grade Levels: Elementary through high school

For further information consult: www.bigchalk.com/
www.field-guides.com/
score.rims.k12.ca.us/virtproj.html

 Spotlight On: Flex Classes

Description. One of the greatest frustrations that talented students face is finding enough time in their school day to enroll in all the classes and activities in which they are interested. It is not unusual for these students to be talented in a number of areas and to have an interest in developing them all. There are never enough hours in the day. A flex class is one solution. Under one scheme, schools offer an independent study option in which the students may enroll. Students who are interested must have the formal endorsement of their teachers. When procured, they make formal application. If admitted (approximately 1% of the student body are), the student can then approach each of their teachers and negotiate the requirements of the class they teach. Students may only attend for exams, participate in the labs, competency out, or be asked to attend the class, as would other students. If time is freed, they can use the time to take another class at the same period, conduct original research, be a lab assistant, attend topical seminars, work on the yearbook, volunteer as a Junior Great Books leader, enroll in classes at the local university, participate in a distance learning class, do community service, or other projects acceptable to the flex class advisor. Under this structure, then, talented students can accelerate their progress through high school and potentially graduate early. At the least, they can construct a program that is more conducive to their individual talent profiles. It is essential that a program of this type receive the endorsement of the board of education prior to initiation, as there are policy considerations that need to be addressed. The greatest of these may be the early graduation policy. With this program, it is not outside of reason that participants could amass the number of credits needed to graduate a semester or year early.

Figure 5.18
Spotlight On:
Flex Classes

Serving Talented Students Through:

	Minimum		Maximum
Accelerated content			
In-depth immersion in topics			
Exploration of interests			

LoS Level: 4

Grade Level: High school

For further information consult: B. Parke. (1995). Developing Curricular Interventions for the Gifted. In J. L. Genshaft, M. Bierely, & C. L. Hollinger (Eds.), *Serving Gifted and Talented Students: A Resource for School Personnel.* Austin, TX: Pro-Ed.

 19   Spotlight On: Foreign Exchange Programs

Description. There is no better way to learn another culture than through immersion. Foreign exchange programs are one way to accomplish this goal. By traveling to another country or by hosting a student from another country, in-depth understanding can be achieved. There are a number of agencies that sponsor these programs. Perhaps the best known is American Field Services. This nonprofit agency takes applications and matches students to families in fifty countries throughout the world. More than 10,000 students (ages 16 to 18) are placed each year through this organization. What is not as readily known, is that programs are also available for older students wishing to engage in international service projects or business and teachers who wish to teach internationally. Programs are available in the sample of countries listed in Table 5.4.

Argentina Canada Czech Republic Germany Italy Turkey	Australia China Denmark Ghana New Zealand United Kingdom	Austria Chile Egypt Hong Kong Norway Venezuela

Table 5.4
Sample Countries With Foreign Exchange Programs

Serving Talented Students Through:

Minimum ← → Maximum

Accelerated content

In-depth immersion in topics

Exploration of interests

Figure 5.19
Spotlight On: Foreign Exchange Programs

LoS Level: 3

Grade Level: High school

For further information consult: B. Hansel. (1993). *The Exchange Student Survival Kit.* Yarmouth, ME: Intercultural Press.
American Field Services at: www.afs.org
Foundation for Foreign Study at: www.effoundation.org/hsyhf.htm

     Spotlight On: Girls and Boys State

Description. Boys and Girls States are civics programs sponsored by the American Legion and the American Legion Auxiliary. Each year, high school students entering their senior year, are selected to attend the event in their state. These programs have involved close to a million students nationwide over the lifetime of the programs. The purpose of Girls and Boys State is to educate youth in the duties and privileges of American citizenship. Attending students are engaged in the same work as political officials. They are immersed in the same duties as are their elected officials at the city, county, and state level. They are elected to political office, form legislative bodies, and work to get bills passed during this one-week simulation. Students can also be nominated for the National Boys and Girls States. Over the week with a federal slant, delegates elect a president and vice president, form a legislative body and hold mock senate hearings, and tour Washington, D.C. By using hands-on experiences, delegates participate in activities designed to give a better understanding about citizenship to American youths, encourage and develop leadership, stimulate Americanism, and instill American traditions. Delegates connect with other delegates who have similar goals and ambitions while also being exposed to diversity and real-world relationships. Many will remember the famous picture of future President Clinton and President Kennedy taken in the rose garden of the White

House. That picture was taken during Bill Clinton's involvement in Boys State. While not all participants in these events become president of the United States, many cite their involvement in these programs as the point at which they decided that service to their community, state, or nation was a career goal.

Figure 5.20
Spotlight On:
Girls and Boys State

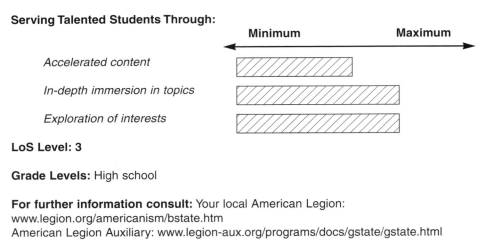

Serving Talented Students Through:

	Minimum	Maximum
Accelerated content		
In-depth immersion in topics		
Exploration of interests		

LoS Level: 3

Grade Levels: High school

For further information consult: Your local American Legion: www.legion.org/americanism/bstate.htm
American Legion Auxiliary: www.legion-aux.org/programs/docs/gstate/gstate.html

 Spotlight On: High School and University Dual Enrollment Programs

Description. Many communities sponsor dual enrollment programs through which high achieving secondary students can attend local institutes of higher education and receive college credit for completing classes. Sponsored by a partnership between the colleges and local school districts, they have been the vehicles through which high school students have completed hundreds of university-level classes. For the most part, schools determine their own standards to determine eligibility. While most students are of junior and senior rank, younger students of exceedingly high ability have also been successful in the programs. Students usually learn about this opportunity through their high school counselors. After they attend an orientation session, they are typically enrolled through regular university registration procedures. Students then attend classes with the university students, receiving the same instruction, schedules of classes, requirements, and grading guidelines. Some high schools offer on-campus sections, using college faculty or their own, when enrollment numbers for any one class are sufficient to merit a designated section. Classes such as psychology, sociology, English, advanced math, and communications are particular favorites. Students who are successful in the program accumulate college credit prior to graduation that they can then apply to their college transcripts. Some participants have garnered credits sufficient to register as sophomores or juniors during their first year in college. Follow-up research (Parke, Nichols, & Brown, 2002) shows that students do not vary significantly from their college classmates in final grades given. Their grade point averages often exceed the grades of freshman-level classmates, indicating that they can be successful students in the courses chosen.

Serving Talented Students Through:

	Minimum	Maximum
Accelerated content		
In-depth immersion in topics		
Exploration of interests		

LoS Level: 4

Grade Levels: High school or middle school (in extreme cases)

For further information consult: www.ipfw.edu/cconnect
Collegiate Connection
IPFW School of Education
2101 E. Coliseum Blvd.
Fort Wayne, IN 46805

  Spotlight On: History Fairs

Description. Staging a history fair can be as simple as asking students to prepare a project on a topic that interests them or assign a project that corresponds with a topic being studied. A more complex fair could correspond with the national history days sponsored by organizations within the United States and Canada. Projects based on themes are very effective in developing student understanding of history and concomitant skills required to be a historian. Such topics as local history, significant people or events, transportation systems, institutions, careers, families, historical antecedents, local heroes, and celebrations are all possible focal points for investigation. Large-scale fairs, such as the U.S. History Day, target students of a certain age, such as grades 6 to 12, and typically have a theme around which students can develop their entries. The theme for the 2002 U.S. History Day was "Revolution, Reaction, Reform in History." The Web site for Florida's History Fair lists advantages that a history fair offers:

- It is a time-tested and successful way to involve students in their history.
- It is a proven vehicle through which teachers accomplish curriculum goals.
- It is student centered, with students directing their own research.
- It is a flexible program, offering students several different ways to enter.
- It is a program in which students win by participating.
- It offers students opportunities to travel widely as they compete. (www.dos.state.fl.us/dhr/museum/fhf.html)

Canada's Heritage Day (www.heritage.k12.nf.ca) has a virtual history fair option in addition to local events for students, schools, businesses, and community organizations, involving five Canadian regions. Fairs may be easily tied into the social studies standards published through the National Council for Social Studies (www.ncss.org).

Figure 5.22
Spotlight On:
History Fairs

Serving Talented Students Through:

	Minimum	Maximum
Accelerated content		
In-depth immersion in topics		
Exploration of interests		

LoS Level: 2

Grade Levels: Elementary through high school

For further information in Canada consult:
www.histori.ca/historica/eng_site/showcase/heritagefairs/index.html

 Spotlight On: Intramural Sports

Description. Most schools sponsor some type of intramural sports program. Schools may offer basketball, volleyball, archery, and gymnastics or lesser-known sports such as broomball or bocce ball. Students self-select participation by simple enrollment and possible fee payment. For the most part, these programs are after school and run for approximately one hour across a predetermined number of weeks. Involvement in this type of program gives participants a chance to develop or hone skills in a sport or to determine if a sport is suited to their tastes and physical abilities. For older students, intramural sports may afford the opportunity to coach or referee sporting events. Doing so gives them a sense of their potential role in the sporting games. It is not unusual to find intramural sports focusing on recreational or leisure sports such as jogging or golfing. Today's physical education curricula are more geared to building these lifelong-leisure athletic skills than in the years past. Following the philosophy that time should be spent readying students for a lifetime of health through exercise, students can use this format for personal growth or career training. For students interested in discovering new sports, intramurals are the perfect format through which they can do that. Students seeking to refine skills can also find the opportunities to do so through intramural sports and coaching as they have extra time to expand their skills.

Figure 5.23
Spotlight On:
Intramural Sports

Serving Talented Students Through:

	Minimum	Maximum
Accelerated content		
In-depth immersion in topics		
Exploration of interests		

LoS Level: 2

Grade Levels: Elementary through high school

For further information consult: J. Byl. (2002). *Intramural Recreation: A Step-by-Step Guide to Creating an Effective Program.* Champaign, IL: Human Kinetics.

Spotlight On: Inventions

Description. Inventing is an exciting alternative for talent development. Students can use their creativity and skills in content areas, higher-order thinking, presentations, and research. Many schools or districts hold their own invention showcase through which teachers at varying levels can begin to include inventions in their curriculum. Students with exceptional inventions may enter them in regionally or nationally sponsored programs (inventors.about.com/cs/younginventors/). Toshiba and the National Science Teachers Association (NSTA) sponsor a large-scale competition, called ExploraVision (K-12), focusing on research and scientific principles (www.education-world.com/a_curr/curr370.shtml), Craftsman Tools and the NSTA also hold a yearly Young Inventors Awards Program (www.nsta.org/programs/craftsman/) open to all students (Grades 2 to 8) in the United States and the U.S. territories. The stated purpose is to challenge students, working independently, to invent or modify a tool using creativity, imagination, science, technology, and mechanical ability. Past winning entries included a stepladder that can be used on uneven surfaces. The popularity of these programs with students, teachers, parents, and communities is so vast that student invention camps are available; they have been featured on television programs and students have patented and sold their inventions. The frustration of designing and developing something new is a great experience for the talented students as they also have the opportunity to develop such personal skills as perseverance, patience, and (for some) strategies for dealing with failure.

Serving Talented Students Through:

	Minimum	Maximum
Accelerated content	////////////	
In-depth immersion in topics	//////////////	
Exploration of interests	//////////////	

Figure 5.24
Spotlight On: Inventions

LoS Level: 2

Grade Levels: Elementary through high school

For further information consult: Kids Invent!
2555 Clovis Avenue
Clovis, CA 93612

 Spotlight On: Jazz Band

Description. The marching band is often the highlight of halftime at Friday night football games. Opening the holiday program is always exciting as the band plays seasonal favorites. Boosters of the band and orchestra programs have resisted the attempt to scale back such programs as they work to find an integral place in school curricula. They strongly argue, and rightfully so, that music programs are not extra but have significant impact on student learning. While there are elementary level programs, most are at the middle and high school level. Many music programs go beyond the large-scale band or orchestra and offer students the opportunity to study specialized music areas. Among the most popular are the competition and jazz bands. Through participation in the jazz band, for example, talented students are exposed to the theory of jazz, its historical roots, unique styling, and personal reactions listeners have to this musical genre. Participation in a jazz band often comes with the opportunity to perform. School-sponsored jazz bands have played at venues ranging from school recitals and events to community programs and weddings. Students not only learn about jazz but also see the impact this musical form has on the broader population. Due to tight budget constraints, students engaged in specialized music instruction and performance must often raise funds to support their study through Band Boosters, bake sales, car washes, and other fund-raising events. These activities allow students to travel to other sites, even internationally, to play and listen to others with the same passion for music. Bands such as jazz bands have represented their school at festivals in their regions, countrywide, and internationally. These ambassadors may have the opportunity to see the world through their involvement with music.

Figure 5.25
Spotlight On:
Jazz Band

Serving Talented Students Through:

	Minimum			Maximum
Accelerated content				
In-depth immersion in topics				
Exploration of interests				

LoS Level: 3

Grade Levels: Middle through high school

For further information consult: For further information consult: H. Burz & K. Marshall. (1999). *Performance-based Curriculum for Music and the Visual Arts: From Knowing to Showing.* Thousand Oaks, CA: Corwin.

 Spotlight On: Junior Achievement

Description. Junior Achievement (JA) is an organization of volunteers that sponsors programs exploring economics and business. Most families have heard the knock at dinnertime and opened the door to find students selling their JA products. JA is much more than a sales organization, however. They sponsor programs specific to the elementary, middle school, and high school grades, each with a scope and sequence. The materials have goals, objectives, and content specific to the targeted level. Elementary-aged students study topics entitled Ourselves, Our Families, Our Community, Our City, Our Region, Our Nation, and Our World. For those students lucky enough to have the appropriate facility available, the culminating activity may be a day at Exchange World, a simulated city with its own government, press, bank, entertainment, and stores. Sixth-grade students spend months in readiness for their day at Exchange City.

Volunteers and teachers are trained in the simulation activities so that students experience the world of commerce first hand. JA materials, available from the national organization, can be implemented at the local level by volunteers. Talented students have the opportunity to engage in career areas of interest in an in-depth manner. Running a city as mayor, editing the Exchange City newspaper, or running a store are experiences with real consequences. An actual paper is produced, items that do not sell at the store are on sale by the end of the day, and it is impossible to find the mayor in her office, as she is likely to be out among her constituents. The middle and high school curricula build on the elementary base and "supplement (the) standard social studies curricula and develop communication skills that are essential to success in the business world" (www.ja.org/).

Serving Talented Students Through:

	Minimum	Maximum
Accelerated content		
In-depth immersion in topics		
Exploration of interests		

Figure 5.26
Spotlight On:
Junior Achievement

LoS Level: 2

Grade Levels: Elementary through high school

For further information consult: Junior Achievement, Inc.
One Education Way
Colorado Springs, CO 80906
press@ja.org

  Spotlight On: Junior Great Books

Description.   The goal of the Great Books programs is to instill in adults and children the habits of mind that characterize a self-reliant thinker, reader, and learner. Great Books programs are predicated on the idea that everyone can read and understand excellent literature—literature that has the capacity to engage the whole person, the imagination as well as the intellect. Participants learn the method of shared inquiry (see Box 5.1) to analyze and discuss their reading selections. Participants think for themselves and learn from each other (talk.greatbooks.org/igb/). The range of selections makes this an excellent choice for talented students as they can easily access materials that are at their levels of reading skills and understanding, employ reasoning skills, engage in spirited discussions through analysis of the selection, or open the opportunity to lead a group. Program leaders, be they teachers, volunteers, librarians, seniors, or students, are trained in the shared-inquiry method and use it to conduct discussions about the readings. Titles included in this commercially available program are carefully chosen and reflect the best of writing for children, adolescents, and adults. Sample titles for young children include: Beatrix Potter's

Tale of Squirrel Nutkin, Rudyard Kipling's *How the Camel Got Its Hump,* and Hans Christian Andersen's *The Emperor's New Clothes*. Content-specific units are also available under the Junior Great Books 'program: *A Gathering of Equals;* the *Declaration of Independence, U.S. Constitution,* and *Bill of Rights;* James Madison's *Federalist No. 10;* Lincoln's *Second Inaugural Address;* and Martin Luther King Jr.'s *Letter from Birmingham Jail* are among the documents that are studied.

Box 5.1

Question Using Shared Inquiry: In *Jack and the Beanstalk,* was it lucky or unlucky for Jack to find the magic beans? Defend your answer by citing references from the story.

Figure 5.27
Spotlight On:
Junior Great Books

Serving Talented Students Through:

	Minimum	Maximum
Accelerated content		
In-depth immersion in topics		
Exploration of interests		

LoS Level: 2/3

Grade Levels: Elementary through high school

For further information consult: The Great Books Foundation
1-800-222-5870

✦28✦   Spotlight On: LEGO League

Description. The FIRST (For Inspiration and Recognition of Science and Technology) LEGO League (www.firstlegoleague.org) is a robotics tournament for children ages 9-14 that combines hands-on, minds-on challenges with a sports-like atmosphere using the LEGO MINDSTORMS Technology a source for talent development? Most decidedly so. Students are joining together in their local areas to participate in LEGO leagues with the purpose of developing projects using these blocks, and entering these projects in competition. Teams consist of up to 10 players and focus on team building, creative problem solving, and analytical thinking. Teams face an annual challenge emulating a real world event or situation and must research, plan, build, program, and test a fully autonomous robot capable of accomplishing the challenge. (LEGO League, www.firstlegoleague.org) A challenge for high school students is available entitled the FIRST Competition. A national competition, it joins high school students with engineers from universities and businesses in an engineering competition. Robotics is used to construct life-sized machines programmed to perform complex tasks. If teams wish, they can take their robots to regional and national competitions. These leagues can be assembled at the local level with or without competition. It is the team building, design, technology, and analytic characteristics of the program that make it so responsive to the needs of talented students. See Box 5.2 for a sample hypothesis activity from the Web site.

Box 5.2   Arctic Impact-Confidential Briefing

Situation: An arctic storm of immense proportions is heading straight for the expedition research site; destruction potential:

Total Annihilation Probable

- Lives at risk due to shifting ice

- Loss of time-sensitive experiments

- Millions of dollars of vital equipment demolished

- Last transmission 9/14/01 at 0600 hours Eastern Standard Time

Calling all FLL Teams for immediate response:

- Analyze data

-Theorize the causes of global climate changes

- Present your findings to a team of judges

SOURCE: LEGO League (www.firstlegoleague.org)

Serving Talented Students Through:

Minimum   Maximum

Accelerated content

In-depth immersion in topics

Exploration of interests

Figure 5.28
Spotlight On:
LEGO League

LoS Level: 2/3

Grade Levels: Elementary through high school

For further information consult: www.lego.com

    Spotlight On: Mental Math

Description. From an informal point of view, mental math is a component of the math curriculum that emphasizes critical thinking as part of math skills. In the formal context, Mental Math is a defined program in which students complete 10 questions a day as part of a rigorous math curriculum that is designed to develop math skills, listening skills, math vocabulary, self-confidence, and motivation. Students in Grades 1 to 5 are expected to develop 50 to 70 math skills through program activities that last no more than 15 minutes per day. Talented students, as other students, receive a number of benefits when engaging in Mental Math. The needed analytic thinking, concentration, motivation, number sense, and confident attitude serve the students both in mathematics and the real world of mathematical application. Here are third-grade questions, from the Math Concepts Web site:

1. What is 718 rounded to the nearest hundred? (700)

2. Write 4,027 in expanded form. (4,000 + 20 + 7)

3. Increase the hundreds place by one in the number 3,560. (3,660) (www.mathconcepts.com/mmintro.html)

Figure 5.29
Spotlight On:
Mental Math

Serving Talented Students Through:

	Minimum	**Maximum**

Accelerated content

In-depth immersion in topics

Exploration of interests

LoS Level: 3

Grade Levels: Elementary through middle school

For further information consult: Math Concepts, Inc
3430 Rimer Road
Concord, NC 28025
1-800-574-9936

 Spotlight On: Mentors

Description. Mentorships are one of the leading strategies for bringing context and excitement to talented students. They are an arrangement between students and, typically, adults for the purpose of giving the students a glimpse into the professional life of the sponsoring mentor. For the most part, these relationships are focused on careers. Students interested in science may be coupled with a researcher. Those interested in healthcare may be working with a doctor, nurse, or therapist. The school, business, or agency of the mentor may sponsor the mentorships. In a wider interpretation of such programs, elementary and middle school students may work with older students, teachers, or community members in mentor relationships. Students have early understanding of the scope and demands of professions of interest. In most circumstances, students actually work in the role with the mentor. In some instances, for example, a student working with a health professional may work for years with the mentor and develop sufficient skill to accompany the mentor into the surgical arena. Students with teachers as mentors may actually teach. Mentors can also serve as guides in matters of educational preparation and relationships as well as careers. It is essential that schools and parents be very judicious in setting up these relationships. Both the mentors and the students should have an agreed-on understanding of the scope and nature of the relationship prior to its inception, to avoid problems based on easily avoidable misconceptions. Unsuccessful pairings can be difficult for both the student and the mentor. When successful, these arrangements can have lifelong positive impact.

Serving Talented Students Through:

Minimum   Maximum

Accelerated content

In-depth immersion in topics

Exploration of interests

Figure 5.30
Spotlight On:
Mentors

LoS Level: 3

Grade Levels: Middle through high school

For further information consult: R. Greene (2000). *The Teenager's Guide to School Outside the Box.* Mansfield Center, CT: Creative Learning Press.
J. Reilly. (1992). *Mentorship.* Mansfield Center, CN: Creative Learning Press.

{31} Spotlight On: Model United Nations

Description. The Model United Nations is a program for high school students interested in the political process, formal and informal debate, and a global point of view. Students gather together at sponsoring sites to spend time engaged in an activity that simulates the United Nations, in New York City, by using role-playing. Students take on the identity of delegates from various nations with allegiances natural to the country's geography, natural resources, and politics. Delegates are immersed in the themes of the experience: multicultural education, interdependence, and international opinion. The Model United Nations Web site (www.ummun. org/), sponsored by the University of Michigan, states,

> By delving into their roles as diplomats to the U.N., students gain a hands-on understanding of the intricacies of world diplomacy. Students are given the opportunity to see international relations in action, a far more exciting and comprehensive learning experience than any textbook or lecture can provide.

For districts that seek to provide an experience within an affordable and accessible format, multiple schools can sponsor activities over a weekend or school year. Students attending these programs have an unusual opportunity to view the world from an intimate point of view. Working to gain multicountry consensus, understanding of world issues, development of the skills needed for persuasion and consensus building, and research skills used to uncover the intimate details of life in their adopted countries gives the students an unparalleled experience in international understanding.

Figure 5.31
Spotlight On:
Model United Nations

Serving Talented Students Through:

	Minimum	Maximum

Accelerated content

In-depth immersion in topics

Exploration of interests

LoS Level: 3

Grade Levels: High school

For further information consult:
Model U.N. for Everyone (Video VHS). *New* York: United Nations Publications.
www.ummun.org or www.amun.org/

   Spotlight on: Opening Night

Description. Plays, be they backyard productions, front-room dance recitals, school shows, or community theater, require more than just acting skills. The talents needed to mount a production are varied. Activities such as directing, painting scenery, finding props, dancing, performing the music, acting, costuming, composing, marketing, stocking refreshments, and producing are all part of theater. Each job has its own requirements and talents from which children must draw. Many parents relate that one of the highlights of their children's developmental years was being invited into the basement to see a show. It may have been a version of a well-known fairytale or a dancing review that resurrects the costumes from last year's dance recital. School productions, ranging from the kindergarten holiday program to the eighth-grade production of a Shakespearean classic to the high school talent show based on a Broadway musical, are also vehicles through which students can gain confidence, showcase their talents, and have real-world evaluation of their work. Theater makes a perfect vehicle through which talented students can balance their academic activities with artistic expression. The talents required to mount a production are so varied, it is next to impossible to find a talent area that is not drawn on through the artistic expressions showcased through drama. Children and youth of all ages can participate at their own level of development with joy and success. Parent volunteers and teacher advisors are to be assured that their contributions to the process will be richly rewarded as they sit as audience and experience the richness of student-mounted theater.

Serving Talented Students Through:

Figure 5.32
Spotlight On:
Opening Night

	Minimum	Maximum
Accelerated content	▨	
In-depth immersion in topics	▨▨▨▨▨▨▨▨▨	
Exploration of interests	▨▨▨▨▨▨▨▨▨	

LoS Level: 2

Grade Levels: Elementary through high school

For further information consult: L. Bany-Winers (1997). *Theater Games and Activities for Kids.* Chicago: Chicago Review Press.
D. Grote & A. Zapel (Eds.). (1998). *Play Directing in the School: A Drama Director's Survival Guide.* Colorado Springs, CO: Meriwether Publishing.

 Spotlight On: Original Research

Description. It may be surprising to consider original research as a program that can be successfully implemented with students throughout the K-12 structure. Parents know that their children begin the process of investigation at a very young age. Investigations are the essence of how children develop and learn. Families delight in remembering experimentation gone awry. Stories of chemistry sets exploding, lab mice getting loose during Thanksgiving dinner, and brewing concoctions in the closet are fondly related at family get-togethers years later. Sometimes it takes those intervening years to find the humor in the situations! Original research at the elementary level can take the form of independent studies, science experiments, or casual exploration. Why does the celery stalk turn red when sitting over night in water turned red with food coloring? How is it that balloons stick to the wall when first rubbed on hair? Even at the earliest elementary grades, students can begin the scientific method by posing questions, hypothesizing, observing for change, developing conclusions, and documenting their observations and recommendations. Students at the middle and high school levels should be encouraged to be researchers on an ongoing basis. Keeping logs of research questions and activities is a prime way to encourage the development of the scientific method as well as higher-order thinking skills. While all students will benefit from being researchers, students talented in this area will find the freedom to go beyond the typical problems and extend their investigations to the more complex questions that make them wonder. Displaying work and presenting findings through school-sponsored research journals, presentations, or professional scientific journals are the steps that take simple investigation to research. That critical step is what makes this activity so fitting for the talented student.

Serving Talented Students Through:

Figure 5.33
Spotlight On:
Original Research

	Minimum	Maximum
Accelerated content	▨▨▨▨▨▨▨	
In-depth immersion in topics	▨▨▨▨▨▨▨▨	
Exploration of interests	▨▨▨▨▨▨▨	

LoS Level: 2/3/4 (depending on nature and scope of research)

Grade Levels: Elementary through high school

For further information consult: C. Nottage & M. Morse. (2000). *IIM: Independent Investigation Method Teacher Manual (K-12)*. Epping, NH: Active Learning Systems.

 Spotlight On: Outdoor Education

Description. Outdoor or environmental education provides the wonders and intricacies of nature as the backdrop for learning. Within the structure of a school curriculum, community-sponsored activity, or family camping trip, outdoor education is a pursuit that can begin the appreciation of nature that can last a lifetime. It is not unusual for students with broad talents to be so immersed in their academic pursuits, or saddled with a misperception of outdoor education as solely sporting and leisure activities, that outdoor education is not a priority. By starting at an early age, they can see outdoor education for what it is—an adventure in discovering and making sense of the world's mysteries. School programs are becoming more abundant as outdoor education is interspersed within the science curriculum and recreation activities. Students can be engaged in such programs as Outward Bound (www.outwardbound.org), class trips to nature camps, environment-based learning labs, and outdoor-activity days sponsored by science education students from a local university. The Association for Environmental and Outdoor Education (www.aeoe.org/) and Project WET (www.montana.edu/wwwwet) are two resources for those wishing to bring outdoor-education programs into the classrooms. These and other environmental programs are based on the standards that have defined best practice since 1978. Written at the first intergovernmental conference on the topic, the Tbilisi Declaration lists three principles:

1. To foster clear awareness of, and concern about, economic, social, political, and ecological interdependence in urban and rural areas

2. To provide every person with opportunities to acquire the knowledge, values, attitudes, commitment, and skills needed to protect and improve the environment

Figure 5.34
Spotlight On:
Outdoor Education

Serving Talented Students Through:

	Minimum	Maximum
Accelerated content	▨▨▨	
In-depth immersion in topics	▨▨▨▨▨	
Exploration of interests	▨▨▨▨	

LoS Level: 2

Grade Levels: Elementary through high school

For further information consult: www.epa.gov/enviroed

3. To create new patterns of behavior of individuals, groups, and society as a whole toward the environment (www.gdrc.org/uem/ee/tbilisi.htm)

This bridge from standards to practice ensures implementers that outdoor educational experiences are curricularly sound and personally rewarding for students.

 Spotlight On: Parenting Classes

Description. Parents are in a better position to assist their children in making decisions about their education when they are informed about the options available for developing talent. Mounting parent classes is one way to address this need. School-sponsored professional development can easily be made available to parents. When professional development programs are designed, including parents in the planning and implementation phases can make these experiences compatible with parental needs. Inviting parents can give them the chance to attend a program that may lead to a greater understanding of their talented children's academic and personal needs. Parents can also take responsibility by seeking out information and experiences that will heighten their awareness of how to best parent talented children. Attending conferences, listening to speakers, watching videos, reading books, observing classes, talking with other parents, seeking out advocacy groups, and leading student activities are all strategies that can be helpful. Involving parents in learning opportunities can be very easy. When sponsoring a community-based Saturday school for talented students, program organizers might offer a class for parents to learn about talent. For the most part, parents waiting for their children to complete their classes, sit in the lounge or cars. During that time, for example, classes can be offered for the parents on topics related to parenting talented children or pertinent videos can be run using a television in the lounge. Such simple options can be easily mounted and are a valuable learning opportunity for the parents. Topics such as creativity, characteristics of talented children, programming, sibling issues, time management, independent investigations, and working with your school can be discussed.

Serving Talented Students Through:

	Minimum	Maximum
Accelerated content	/////////////	
In-depth immersion in topics	/////////////////	
Exploration of interests	/////////////////	

Figure 5.35
Spotlight On:
Parenting Classes

LoS Level: NA

Grade Levels: Elementary through high school parents

For further information consult: S. Rimm. (2001). *Keys to Parenting the Gifted Child.* Hauppauge, NY: Barron's Educational Series.
J. Saunders & P. Espeland. (1991). *Bringing out Their Best: A Resource Guide for Parents of Young Gifted Children* (2nd ed.). Minneapolis, MN: Freespirit Publishing.

Spotlight On: Peer Mediation

Description. Peer mediation is a structured process for conflict resolution. When used in schools, students are trained to act as mediators for disputes and conflicts involving other students. Their goal is to assist in finding constructive alternatives to the problems students are facing. In order to do so, student-selected peer mediators are trained in techniques geared to problem finding and problem solving, such as active listening and issue clarification. Mediators, supervised by schools' faculty members, assist disputants in finding reasonable and mutually acceptable solutions to the conflict that precipitated the mediation. Mediators ask the disputants to explain the situation, after which they ask questions and assist the disputants in finding solutions. Typical mediation steps are to agree on ground rules, tell stories, verify stories, discuss stories, generate solutions, discuss solutions, select a solution, and sign a contract for future behavior. While not all problems are appropriate for resolution through this forum, many school issues are. Frequent topics for mediation include name-calling, bullying, rumors, and recess disputes. Problems found in elementary schools are usually of less intensity then those presented in high schools. Thus elementary-aged mediators are able to deal with the types of problems they are faced with, as the problems are familiar. If a problem is outside the scope of what the students can reasonably mediate, normal school disciplinary solutions are employed. School-based programs report improvements in positive outcomes for conflict resolution, declines in student conflicts and violence, reduced absenteeism, more time on task in classrooms, and more sustained instructional time.

Figure 5.36
Spotlight On:
Peer Mediation

Serving Talented Students Through:

	Minimum	Maximum
Accelerated content		
In-depth immersion in topics		
Exploration of interests		

LoS Level: 2

Grade Levels: Elementary through high school

For further information consult: Conflict Resolution/Peer Mediation Research Project: University of Florida at www.coe.ufl.edu/CRPM/CRPMhome.html
Teacher Talk: www.iapeace.org

   Spotlight On: Power of the Pen

Description. Power of the Pen is a not-for-profit program, started in 1986, for middle school students interested in writing. At this time, it operates only in Ohio. Student writing is the basis for competitions at the district, regional, and state levels. Schools assemble teams of students who prepare for the competition by developing their skills through direct instruction and impromptu writing. During team registration, a packet of program information is sent to each team. From this packet, teams prepare for the competitions. When the competition is engaged, students use expressive writing to develop impromptu pieces. Students who excel at the highest levels are given awards. Team achievement is also rewarded. As many as one third of the schools eligible in Ohio participate in this program. This numbers over 10,000 students per year. Team coaches are also involved in a support network. From this group, they receive information on instructional and team-building strategies for collaboration and writing. Team coaches are required as they also serve as competition judges. Students get immediate feedback on their writing at all phases of the program. By involvement in this program, students are reported to develop greater abilities in the areas of critical thinking, creative thinking, and writing skill. A strong community support component is included.

Serving Talented Students Through:

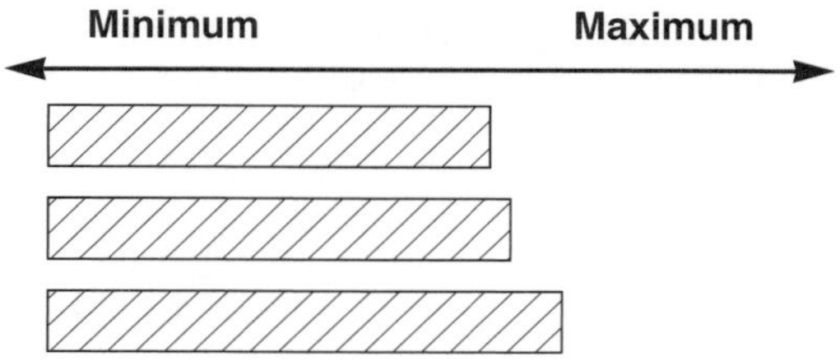

Figure 5.37
Spotlight On:
Power of the Pen

Minimum **Maximum**

Accelerated content

In-depth immersion in topics

Exploration of interests

LoS Level: 3

Grade Level: Middle school

For further information consult: www.powerofthepen.org/pop/pop.htm
Loraine B. Merrill, Executive Director
Power of the Pen
Box 442
Richfield, Ohio 44286

38 Spotlight On: Problem-Based Learning

Description. Problem-based learning (PBL) is a system of instruction through which "ill-structured" problems are the basis for learning and developing skills in critical thinking, team building, self-directed learning, and problem solving. Problems are chosen that develop these skills as they are being investigated. The system begins with teachers posing authentic problems for student teams to solve. As skills are developed, students take an increasingly greater role, with teachers serving as coaches, evaluators, or resources to the students. A problem on which learning centers

- Is ill-structured in nature
- Is met as a "messy" situation
- Often changes with the addition of new information
- Is not solved easily or formulaically
- Does not always result in a "right" answer (Rhem, 1998)

Program participants report that positive student outcomes can be found in the areas of motivation and higher-order thinking skills. Talented students are encouraged to develop their abilities through the engagement of

Figure 5.38
Spotlight On:
Problem-Based
Learning

Serving Talented Students Through:

	Minimum	Maximum
Accelerated content		
In-depth immersion in topics		
Exploration of interests		

LoS Level: 1

Grade Levels: Elementary through high school

For further information consult: W. J. Stepien. (2001). *The Internet and Problem-Based Learning: Developing Solutions Through the Web.* Tucson, AZ: Zephyr Press. L. Torp & S. Sage. (1998). *Problems as Possibilities: Problem-Based Learning for K–12 Education.* Alexandria, VA: Association for Supervision & Curriculum Development.

problems that are pertinent to the talent areas they display. When students assume the role of problem solvers and teachers assume the role of tutors and coaches:

- Information is shared but knowledge is a personal construction of the learner.
- Thinking is fully articulated and held to strict benchmarks.
- Assessment is an authentic companion to the problem and process.
- The PBL unit is not necessarily interdisciplinary in nature but is always integrative. (Rhem, 1998)

 Spotlight On: Professional Development

Description. One of the best strategies for meeting the needs of talented students is pairing them with an excellent teacher. Knowing how to ask divergent questions, managing multiple-ability levels within a classroom, daring to take risks, understanding the needs of this population, and being content area specialists are just a few of the skills needed to work effectively with these students. To develop the high level of skill needed to effectively engage talented students, professional development is generally needed, as it is difficult to develop these skills in a preservice teacher-training program. It takes time to fully develop this art of teaching. However, it can be done, and professional development is a necessary part of the process. There are many activities that can be part of a professional development plan. University classes, conferences, visitations, journal and magazine articles, co-teaching, action research, demonstrations, master teachers, content-specific or process-based training, online chats, interviews, and videotapes can all provide new insight into teaching techniques that can be useful in establishing a learning environment conducive to developing teaching techniques that may lead to talent development. School districts sponsor professional-development opportunities, but they rarely include the types of in-depth skill development needed to reach this goal. It may be necessary to go beyond the school-sponsored activities and locate alternative activities that address this concern. Recommended topics include

- Aspects of intelligence
- Managing the classroom for multiple-ability levels
- Working with parents to maximize student achievement
- Active-research strategies
- Content-specific instructional strategies
- Consultation and collaboration skills
- Understanding descriptive and inferential statistics

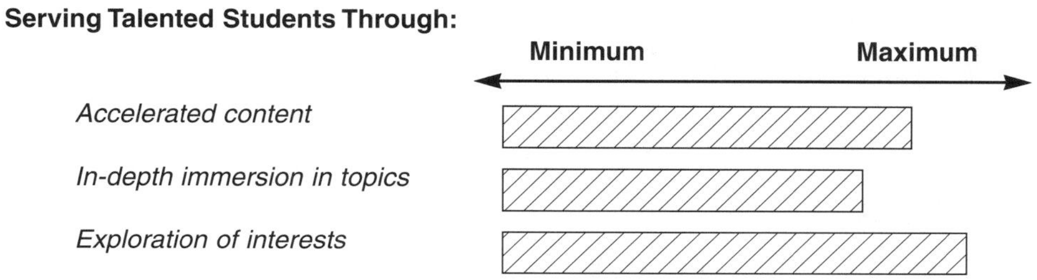

Serving Talented Students Through:

Minimum   Maximum

Accelerated content

In-depth immersion in topics

Exploration of interests

Grade Levels: Elementary through high school teachers

For further information consult: P. Dettmer (1990). *Staff Development for Gifted Programs: Putting It Together and Making It Work*. Washington, DC: Service Publications.

Figure 5.39
Spotlight On:
Professional
Development

   Spotlight On: Quiz Bowl

Description. Quiz Bowl competitions are regularly found in listings of programs for gifted and talented students. While any student may audition and participate, the program is one that serves talented students well. This population of students often exhibits vast arrays of knowledge across many disciplines. As Quiz Bowls are based on broad academic skills, this is a natural match. Participation in this program enhances the learning of talented students through requiring study skills, developing systems for memorization, taking part in a competition format, studying a wide range of topics, building team skills, and expanding an understanding of responsibility. For the most part, students get a great deal of satisfaction from the preparation and competition phases of this program. While Quiz Bowl programs are typical at the college and high school levels, middle and elementary school students also enjoy the challenge and should be included in the quiz bowl format. Interschool competition is typical but not essential to the process. Competitions between grade levels, classes, reading groups, or teachers and students can engender a great deal of enthusiasm. Bowls organized on specific topics can also be effective. Decimals, states and capitals, chemical symbols, nouns and verbs, world history, Spanish vocabulary, human body systems, musical notes, or current events can all be topics for generating questions. Students can also sponsor the events and write questions in preparation for the events. They not only get the experience of organizing such an event, they also receive the benefit of delving into information on the topics to be covered. Here are sample questions for an elementary school event:

1. What mineral is added to milk for bone development?

2. Add the figures 46 + 25 + 87 + 13 + 74.

3. In which city is the Liberty Bell?

4. Name three new countries previously part of the USSR.

5. What gas is emitted from plants?

6. Who is secretary general of the United Nations?

Figure 5.40
Spotlight On:
Quiz Bowl

Serving Talented Students Through:

Minimum   Maximum

Accelerated content

In-depth immersion in topics

Exploration of interests

LoS Level: 3

Grade Levels: Elementary through high school

For further information consult: www.mindfun.com
                                       Questions Unlimited
                                       P.O. Box14798
                                       Columbus, OH 43214

 Spotlight On: Reenactments

Description. Bringing history to life through reenactments is a memorable way to study the past. The in-depth study and creativity it takes to stage one is poignant for the students who take part. Under the sponsorship of teachers, school clubs, community and national organizations, or neighborhood groups, students can become the historical figures they play. The complexity of the event may vary based on the age of the participants and available resources. The extent of planning needed also varies due to available resources, age of students, targeted authenticity, numbers of people involved, and availability of partnerships with other organizations. Participation in the actual reenactment can be very exciting for the students involved. We must not overlook the advantage of being involved in the planning. There is a long list of tasks that need to be completed before the actual event. It is the research involved in fulfilling these tasks that leads to vast learning possibilities. What did the soldiers in the Civil War eat? What is a musket? Where did the Oregon Trail begin? How was armor for horses constructed? How did they get the armor onto the horses? (See Table 5.5 for three Web sites featuring information about reenactments.) The questions to be answered are extensive. Just knowing what questions to ask is a task in itself. Surely, the team effort needed to mount a reenactment will lead students to a better understanding of the challenges faced by their predecessors.

Topic	URL
Civil War	www.thehistorynet.com/calendar/reenactments.htm
Medieval Time	www.regina.org/
Oregon Trail	www.webinstruct.net/webquest/trail/t_process.html

Table 5.5
Sample
Reenactments

Serving Talented Students Through:

Minimum   Maximum

Accelerated content

In-depth immersion in topics

Exploration of interests

LoS Level: 1

Grade Levels: Elementary through high school

For further information consult: S. F. Roth. (1998).*Past Into Present: Effective Techniques for First-Person Historical Interpretation*. Chapel Hill, NC: University of North Carolina Press.

Figure 5.41
Spotlight On:
Reenactments

 42   Spotlight On: Science Fair

Description. Science projects are a classic part of the curriculum for most schools. As early as kindergarten, students and their parents are engaged in the activities that result in the display, research papers, and presentations that make up a science project. Students may study butterflies, consider the difference between color and light, examine the preferences of their classmates as they conduct a taste test of varying colas, and trace back the bloodlines of their prize cattle. Some science fairs are totally optional, and the work is done exclusively at home. Other fairs are part of the school requirements and are graded as such. Virtual fairs are also available, as are community, regional, state, and national events. For the young scientist, this is an excellent way to learn the scientific method. Typical steps (www. scifair.org/) in developing a science project appear in Table 5.6. Internet sites and resources abound. A sampling of Web sites appears in Table 5.7.

Serving Talented Students Through:

Minimum   Maximum

Accelerated content

In-depth immersion in topics

Exploration of interests

LoS Level: 2/3/4 (depending on nature and scope of project)

Grade Levels: Elementary through high school

For further information consult: J. Vancleave. (2000). *Janice Vancleave's Guide to More of the Best Science Projects.* New York: John Wiley.

Figure 5.42
Spotlight On:
Science Fair

Table 5.6
Steps in Preparing
a Science Project

1.	Select a topic.	6.	Analyze your results.
2.	Research your topic.	7.	Write a report.
3.	Make a plan.	8.	Make your display.
4.	Conduct the experiment.	9.	Rehearse your presentation.
5.	Observe what happens.	10.	Do your best.

Table 5.7
Sample Web Sites for
Science Fair
Information

Topic	URL
Project Ideas	physics.usc.edu/ScienceFairs/
Math for Science Fairs	mathforum.org/teachers/mathproject.html
Mad Science	www.madsci.org/experiments/
Resource Guide	www.ipl.org/youth/projectguide/

 43   **Spotlight On: Scouting and Y-Guide Programs**

Description. Vast numbers of people have engaged in a Scouting or Guide program at some point in their lives. These organizations have a long history of providing programs for youth around the world. Beyond the ever-enticing cookies, popcorn, and calendars, such programs challenge the participants in ways that enhance their learning and their lives. The base program structure is made up of activities that lead to badges of attainment for meeting levels of achievement that are preprescribed. Participants at all levels can find activities that correspond to their interests and goals. Along with badge activities, participants engage in others that are designed to build skill and character. Sports, camping, field trips, the arts, cultural exchange, service projects, and environmental stewardship are listed as basis for ongoing program activities. While schools may provide space for these programs, they are typically community based. Scouting is available for people of all ages who meet their membership criteria. Most are familiar with the programs offered for students of elementary and middle school ages. Programs, however, are also available for students in high schools and colleges. Y-Guides are for school-age children and their parents. Adults can also become involved as volunteer troop leaders.

Figure 5.43
Spotlight On:
Scouting and Y-Guide
Programs

Serving Talented Students Through:

Minimum ← → Maximum

Accelerated content

In-depth immersion in topics

Exploration of interests

LoS Level: 2

Grade Levels: Elementary through high school

For further information consult: www.girlscouts.org or www.bsa.scouting.org; www.ymca.net.index.jsp

Spotlight On: Seminars

Description. Seminars can take many forms and serve many purposes for students with talent. They can be a source of new information, skill development, schedule flexibility, community outreach, and advanced learning in many areas. Students at all levels can profit from seminar experiences; however, seminars are most often found in high school schedules. Organizations, schools, businesses, universities, community groups, clubs, and service societies are among the groups that typically organize seminar experiences. For most students, seminars are attended at school as part of a class or as a designated, stand-alone class. Seminars can also be found online or in community education fliers, summer school listings, distance education catalogues, and bulletin boards in the counselor's office at school. Motivated students can readily find topics that correspond to their interests (see Table 5.8). The seminar experience gives talented students an opportunity to discuss targeted topics with others while they investigate topics around which the seminars are based. Their skills of research, analysis, communication, listening, and idea development are among those needed for successful participation in a seminar program. These skills may be developed through, or seen as, prerequisite for program participation.

Topic	URL
Arts	www.slc.edu/summer_programs.html
Martial arts	www.edgekickboxing.com/
Personal development	www.pathofsuccess.org/
Character	www.charactercounts.org
Journalism	www.poynter.org
Holocaust	www.holocausthistory.net

Table 5.8
Sample Web Sites for Seminar Topics

Serving Talented Students Through:

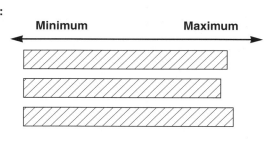

Figure 5.44
Spotlight On: Seminars

LoS Level: 3

Grade Levels: Middle through high school

For further information consult: R. L. Jolles. (2000). *How to Run Presentations and Workshops.* New York: John Wiley.

 Spotlight On: Show Choir

Description. Show Choirs are often a component of a school's music curriculum or an extracurricular activity. As the National Association of Show Choirs, (NASC) states in their mission statement (www.showchoirs. com/), "The NASC seeks to promote and recognize musical, theatrical, and choreographic excellence through the use of standardized measurements of technical and artistic achievement." This combination of music, dance, and theatre makes the Show Choir experience unique. What makes this program excellent for talented students is that it combines so many. Students who participate should be skilled in vocal, dance, and theatrical performance. Show Choir members perform at competitions, school activities, their own recitals, and community events. They are always well received, as the performances are technically complex and spirited. Coaches for these groups are from various disciplines. It would not be unusual to find the students working with the choir director, a local dance teacher or choreographer, and a member of the theater department. Working together, this team of coaches leads students beyond the normal recital fare and into the realm of theatrical performance. The cross-discipline exposure is broadening for talented students and requires higher-order thinking skills to assimilate the breadth of talent from which the coaches draw. Surprisingly, when competing, it is not always the groups with the most financial support or largest student body who are judged superior. Students from settings such as rural areas with small student bodies are just as likely to score well as those from more populated areas. It is the combined talent of the students and coaches that mix to generate outstanding performance.

Figure 5.45
Spotlight On:
Show Choir

Serving Talented Students Through:

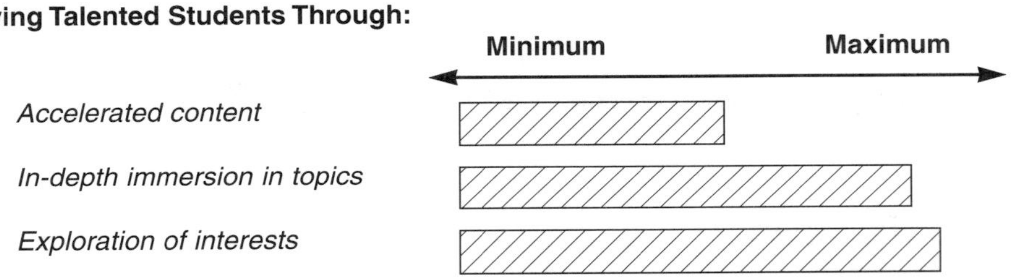

LoS Level: 3

Grade Levels: Middle and high school

For further information consult: P. Gritton. (1999). *Encores for Choirs: 24 Show-Stopping Concert Pieces.* New York: Oxford University Press.

46 Spotlight On: Space Camp

Description. Camp experiences of all sorts can bring challenging learning experiences to students with unusual talent. Schools organize some camping experiences, while others are family decisions. Attending a camping fair always results in surprise at the numbers and types of camping experiences available to children, adults, and families. NASA's Space Camps are just one example. Through this agency, camping experiences are organized for school groups, libraries, community groups such as Scouts, 4H, Junior Reserve Officers Training Corps (JROTC), teachers, and children interested in finding out more about the "great frontier." The Houston site offers day and overnight camps for children beginning at age 4. Even at such a young age, children spend 45 minutes trying on space suits and finding out what astronauts feel all encased in their massive suits. An experience for middle and high school aged students focuses on rocketry and culminates in "liftoffs." U.S. Space Camps (www.spacecamp.com), located in Huntsville, Alabama, offers camps for children and adults as well. This site, in operation since 1982, offers multiple-day programs for campers from around the country. Attendees have the opportunity to work in space simulators, view I-Max films of space on movie screens that are five stories high, feel weightlessness, and work as in a space station. Experiments, rocket building, simulated launches, and lectures on all that is involved in space travel and exploration are featured. For those interested in space, this is a chance to learn the intricacies of the topic while engaging in the same kinds of experiences that astronauts do. For students seeking advanced knowledge, skills, or experiences involving space, such camps offer the activities that will lead to further advancement toward these goals.

Serving Talented Students Through:

	Minimum	Maximum
Accelerated content		
In-depth immersion in topics		
Exploration of interests		

LoS Level: 2

Grade Levels: Kindergarten through high school (depending on site)

For further information consult: NASA at 1-281-283-7722 or the U.S. Space & Rocket Center at 1-800-533-7281.

Figure 5.46
Spotlight On:
Space Camp

47   Spotlight On: Speaker's Bureau

Description. A speaker's bureau listing elementary-aged students, is this likely? Absolutely. Students, regardless of age, are authorities on topics and can function as experts. In order to qualify for inclusion in such a formal or informal listing, students must be well versed in a topic, interested in talking to others about that topic, and willing to develop (or already have developed) public-speaking skills. These students can be consulted for class, school, or community level assignments. Mothers' clubs, PTOs, chambers of commerce, Rotary Clubs, Lions, Retired Teachers Clubs, and the school district administrators are among the potential audiences for the speaker's bureau. It does not take long for novice teachers at any level to quickly learn that there are always students in their classes that know more than they do about some topics. Rather than attempt to maintain the façade of expert on everything, teachers are better advised to harness that knowledge in a useful way. The student who is a computer buff can be the expert for other students and teachers regarding technology. Those who are steeped in knowledge about dinosaurs may be the ideal people to come into a kindergarten to discuss these prehistoric animals. Expertise on volleyball may be the reason a member of the speaker's bureau would be called on to help the coach at a sports camp. By inclusion in this type of program, talented students have the opportunity to share what they know with others, build confidence and self-esteem, represent their school in a positive light, and contribute to the overall expertise of those with whom they work.

Figure 5.47
Spotlight On:
Speaker's Bureau

Serving Talented Students Through:

	Minimum		Maximum

Accelerated content

In-depth immersion in topics

Exploration of interests

LoS Level: 3

Grade Levels: Elementary through high school

For further information consult: D. Parker. (2001). *Roadmap to Confident Basic Public Speaking* (2nd ed.). Philadelphia: Xlibris.

   Spotlight On: Special Olympics

Description. It may be surprising to find a listing for Special Olympics among these programs for talent development. Talented students may have an interest in working with the population of disabled people as a volunteer or coach for this program. The Special Olympics is a well-known program that sponsors athletic competitions in over 150 countries around the world. Athletes come together on a world stage every 4 years, but local competitions are held every year in most locations. In order to be eligible, athletes

> Must be at least 8 years old and identified by an agency or professional as having one of the following conditions: mental retardation, cognitive delays, or significant learning or vocational problems due to cognitive delay that require or have required specially designed instruction. (Retrieved from www.specialolympics.org/)

Organizers assemble the Olympiad by choosing from 26 summer or winter Olympic-type sports. See Table 5.9 for a sample of competitions that may be included.

Athletes live by the motto, "Let me win. But if I cannot win, let me be brave in the attempt." For this program to be a success, it relies on volunteers and coaches who work with the athletes prior to and during the competition. These are the people who make the events successful for the athletes. They have the honor of greeting athletes as they cross the finish lines of their events. There is the potential not only for service but for also an increased understanding of others. For the talented student, Special Olympics provides an opportunity to apply their talents to a very worthwhile activity while further developing the talents which they hold.

Table 5.9
Sports for Special
Olympics
Competitions

Cycling	Roller skating	Tennis
Bowling	Softball	Golf
Floor Hockey	Aquatics	Gymnastics
Team Handball	Power Lifting	Figure Skating

Serving Talented Students Through:

Figure 5.48
Spotlight On:
Special Olympics

	Minimum	Maximum
Accelerated content	▨	
In-depth immersion in topics	▨▨	
Exploration of interests	▨▨▨	

LoS Level: 2

Grade Levels: Elementary through high school

For further information consult: M. Kennedy. (2002). *Special Olympics*. New York: Children's Books.

   Spotlight On: Sports Day

Description. Grandstands are full of parents and grandparents looking out to the field filled with students wearing T-shirts of every color denoting the grade level and classroom they represent. The students run the 440 relay, up and over relay, soccer ball skills event, and 911 team relay—among many other events—and they cheer for their teammates. The hours spent in the stadium are valuable as they are consumed by rapt attention and competition that pushes even the most-talented athletes to reach for their highest performance level. The anonymity of a field full of students allows the less talented to also do their best without concern for appearing inept. As the field of physical education moves to one based more on leisure education, physical educators are concentrating on imparting skills that students can use throughout their lives in order to stay physically fit. More emphasis is on such skills as wall climbing, swimming, table tennis, jogging, archery, and hiking. Sports days, then, have the potential of including a wide range of activities that have a greater possibility of including sports at which students find a reasonable level of proficiency. At the same time, sports days may include traditional events (running, throwing, shooting) at which the more-talented athletes can also participate at a level that reflects their innate abilities. For the most part, the more activities included, the more likely it is that students can engage in at least one event that gives them the opportunity to participate at a high level.

Serving Talented Students Through:

Figure 5.49
Spotlight On:
Sports Day

	Minimum	Maximum
Accelerated content	▨	
In-depth immersion in topics	▨▨▨	
Exploration of interests	▨▨▨	

LoS Level: 1

Grade Levels: Elementary through high school

For further information consult:
T. K. Smith & N. G. Cestaro. (1998). *Student-Centered Physical Education: Strategies for Developing Middle School Fitness and Skills.* Champaign, IL: Human Kinetics Publishers.
K. Lumsdea & S. Jones. (1996). *Ready-to-Use Secondary P.E. Activities Program: Lessons, Tournaments and Assessments for Grades 6-12.* Upper Saddle River, NJ: Prentice Hall.

    Spotlight On: Student Council

Description. While we typically think of student council as a high school activity, more middle schools and elementary schools are initiating these programs. Elementary students are meeting weekly to sponsor community service programs and serve as advisors to the principal. Middle school students add to the responsibilities of the elementary students by sponsoring social events for their classmates. High school students may go yet a step further and study leadership and civics as part of the responsibilities they embrace. Under some circumstances, high schools make student council a class in addition to a service organization. In this case, students are involved daily in the workings of the school, student activities, and study of such topics as leadership development, civics, handling stress, government, and *Robert's Rules of Order* (www.robertsrules.com/). For talented students, student council may be one of the only organizations through which leadership skills and teamwork can be developed. Students can participate at different levels. Students who wish to be integrally involved may run for election to the group or within the group for office. If election is not realized or student council is not an elected office, students talented in leadership skills (or those seeking development of leadership skills) may volunteer to head committees that serve school functions. Homecoming, bake sales, dance committees, spirit groups, food drives, clubs, boosters, and service projects are among the many activities that need direction and are opportunities to develop leadership. Talented students should be encouraged to do so.

Figure 5.50
Spotlight On:
Student Council

Serving Talented Students Through:

	Minimum	Maximum
Accelerated content	▨	
In-depth immersion in topics	▨▨▨▨▨▨	
Exploration of interests	▨▨▨▨▨	

LoS Level: 2

Grade Levels: Elementary through high school

For further information consult: The guidance counselor or administrator at your local school.

Spotlight On: Student Newspaper

Description. Editing, writing, funding, and marketing the school newspaper begins the passion for journalism that many students take into careers. For students talented in the areas required for a successful newspaper, generating their school papers can hone skills that can be applied to other classes or activities. Writing for a newspaper requires talents beyond writing. Journalists must also have an interest in the community at large and the events that surround them. It is the pairing of these interests with the talent in writing, editing, and marketing that combine to make a talented journalist. Student newspapers are popular at the middle and elementary school levels. It is obvious when reading these papers that students, even at an early age, can have substantial talent in this area. School-sponsored newspapers are not the only papers to which students can contribute. Camps, swim teams, neighborhoods, bowling leagues, classrooms, and families can all have newspapers. With great amount of publishing software available, distributing content to others has become easy. One of the most exciting uses of the Internet is family communication. Keeping in touch with family members can become a simple matter of assembling a format, writing the latest family news, and attaching the product to an email addressed to those who will be interested in its content. Some families simply add their comments to the newsletter they receive and then send it on to the next family. This same strategy can be used to connect organizations, church groups, family reunion attendees, or friends. The talented student can be the monitor for this activity. It is never too early to develop the skills needed to write. Any vehicle that encourages writing should be valued highly. School and community-sponsored newspapers are just one such medium.

Serving Talented Students Through:

	Minimum	Maximum
Accelerated content		
In-depth immersion in topics		
Exploration of interests		

Figure 5.51
Spotlight On:
Student Newspaper

LoS Level: 2

Grade Levels: Elementary through high school

For further information consult: D. Crosby & L. Britt. (1999). *Create Your Own Class Newspaper: A Complete Guide for Planning, Writing, and Publishing a Newspaper*. Nashville, TN: Incentive Publications.

 Spotlight On: Summer Stars

Description. The Summer Stars Program (Cantrell & Edbon, 1997) is based on Gardner's multiple intelligence (MI) model. This camp program, sponsored by New Canaan (CT) Public Schools, is for students ages 7 to 12 and involves both student-selected activities and internships. Keeping true to Gardner's theories, each student has a different schedule for any given day, as each is unique in abilities and aspirations. Among the projects a student could choose have been "producing a handcrafted bound book; writing musical compositions, constructing rockets, building block structures for students' blueprints, writing and illustrating the camp newsletter, and reinventing stories to tell at the closing ceremony" (p. 38). In addition, students keep a daily journal, and parent education is a priority. All parents receive information about the MI model prior to the beginning of camp. The structure and content of this type of camp experience is conducive to the learning of talented children and youth. First, options are available from which to choose. Next, flexibility allows the campers to focus on the content areas they select and learn through the modality they prefer. Keeping a daily journal employs the reflective skills that are essential to higher-order thinking and is essential for analysis. Planning for daily activities places the responsibility for learning where it belongs, on the campers. Last, parents are given information from which to support the camp's philosophical base and their children's work. Such programs are adaptable to other settings and sponsors. School districts, community organizations, service clubs, and universities can all mount this model for adventure with great possibility of success.

Figure 5.52
Spotlight On:
Summer Stars

Serving Talented Students Through:

	Minimum	Maximum

Accelerated content

In-depth immersion in topics

Exploration of interests

LoS Level: 2/3 (depending on program)

Grade Levels: Elementary through middle school

For further information consult: M. L. Cantrell & S. A. Edbon. (1997). The Summer Stars Program. *Educational Leadership, 55*(1), 38-42

 Spotlight On: Sustained Silent Reading

Description. Sustained silent reading (SSR) is a program used throughout the country to encourage reading. Students in all grades can benefit from this program that puts a premium on reading books for the joy of it. Sometimes called DEAR (Drop Everything and Read), at designated times, all classroom instruction ends and students pick up self-selected books to read. When done right, teachers, aides, principals, cafeteria workers, and others read as well. By so doing, students observe the value of reading as well as enjoy their books. SSR can be implemented in many ways. A single teacher can use the technique or an entire school may have a simultaneous SSR time. Most participants use SSR daily or many times a week rather than sporadically. This is not to say that SSR cannot be used now and then, only that it is far more effective when done on a regularly scheduled basis. Some sites put aside one SSR time a week for oral reading. Either a teacher or student selects a book to read to the class. For others, one or two chapters are read at a time. SSR should not be seen as an elementary program. Middle school and high school students can also profit from regular SSR. There is no agreement on whether students should be engaged in a book-related activity as part of the SSR time. Some teachers require journals while others group students for book talks. For many, the goal is reached by simply having students read for sheer enjoyment. It is the position of many teachers that students should have this time to read without any obligation for additional activity. Whatever the structure, giving students the time to enjoy reading a book at their own level of skill and interest is a precursor to lifelong reading habits and a wonderful opportunity for talented readers to immerse themselves in a medium they enjoy.

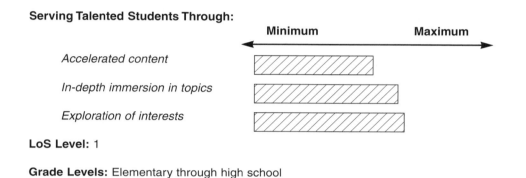

Serving Talented Students Through:

Minimum   Maximum

Accelerated content

In-depth immersion in topics

Exploration of interests

LoS Level: 1

Grade Levels: Elementary through high school

For further information consult: www.education-world.com/acurr/curr038.shtml

Figure 5.53
Spotlight On:
Sustained Silent
Reading

 Spotlight On: Talent Shows

Description. Almost everyone has been in a talent show at one time or another. Perhaps it was in a backyard or on the school stage. Wherever it was, you are likely to remember the butterflies that filled your stomach just before your performance. These events go a long way toward perfecting how talent is expressed. Talent shows require the collaboration of many people with various talents in order to be successful. Participants need to locate the talent, publicize the event, provide music, perform, sell tickets, and more. The team, not just one performer, makes for a successful show. When youths stage such an event, they are taking their talents public and asking for others to witness what they can do. This takes a level of risk that not all people are willing to chance. For the talented, this alone is a strong motive for arranging a talent show. Many talented youths are afraid to publicly display what they can do for fear of rejection. The earlier this fear can be faced, the more quickly one can gain confidence in one's abilities. Talent shows can display a wide range of acts. Simultaneous art fairs can further extend the number of people who can participate. Dancers, potters, singers, painters, woodcarvers, pianists, ventriloquists, orators, weavers, jewelers, and guitarists can all be included. In order to offer the best possible experience, it is essential that the participants be required to practice their part, as the discipline of the performance is an outcome possible only under this condition. Schools, churches, service clubs, homeowners associations, or the three children next door are among the groups that can sponsor talent shows. Regardless of the venue, it is the opportunity to display one's abilities to others that makes this type of event so important to talent development.

Figure 5.54
Spotlight On:
Talent Shows

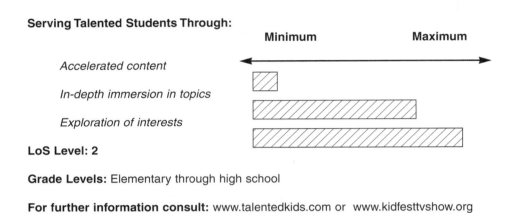

Serving Talented Students Through:

	Minimum	Maximum
Accelerated content		
In-depth immersion in topics		
Exploration of interests		

LoS Level: 2

Grade Levels: Elementary through high school

For further information consult: www.talentedkids.com or www.kidfesttvshow.org

⁙55⁙ Spotlight On: Tarheel Museum

Description. Touring museums is an activity that school classes and families often do. It is exciting to see the art, history, artifacts, and relics that can be viewed. To extend this activity to a more-personal level, having youth make their own museums is a natural extension. Talented students often like to make collections. Parents report finding stacks of stones, trading cards, or butterflies mixed in with various odds and ends of their children's possessions. Bringing order to the collections is what moving them into a museum context can do. Acting as a curator for collections in the museum is a task that involves looking at the artifacts, choosing the best, and displaying them in a way that others can appreciate. Passe and Whitley (1998) report on such a museum created by fourth graders in North Carolina. The Tarheel Museum was placed in their school's media center. Teachers drew on the academic standards of finding and organizing information to justify the vast amount of time needed to assemble the museum. Teachers identified the projects that were to be included in the museum and asked students to sign up for the one they wished to complete. Small groups were identified to work on each project. Students were assigned to interview local people, design the exhibit, complete needed art, and do other tasks that became necessary as the museum developed. Talent was drawn on from many students in many ways as a variety of tasks were needed; it becomes easy to pair tasks with students of corresponding ability. Volunteering for those of greatest interest allows students to develop talent in a way that contributes to a worthwhile project.

Serving Talented Students Through:

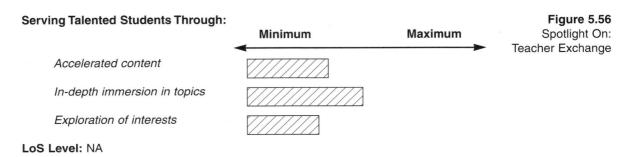

Minimum   Maximum

Accelerated content

In-depth immersion in topics

Exploration of interests

Figure 5.55
Spotlight On:
Tarheel Museum

LoS Level: 1/3 (depending on specific contribution)

Grade Levels: Elementary through middle school

For further information consult: J. Passe & I. Whitley. (1998). The *Best* Museum for Kids? The One They Build Themselves! *Social Studies, 89*(4), 183-186.

 Spotlight On: Teacher Exchange

Description. One method of professional development, used to enrich the skills and interests of teachers working with highly talented students, is to organize a formal teacher exchange program. Under this model, teachers switch teaching assignments with others also interested in this process. By so doing, they have the opportunity to experience other work environments and learn from other teachers and sites. One popular variation includes teachers from urban and rural areas. When they exchange, each is immersed in totally different settings that can then inform their teaching. We often hear about diversity and its importance for students to understand. There is no better way to develop the insight needed for these discussions than through actual work experience in differing places. Such programs, typically organized through a school district's central office, may also be sponsored by a university or intermediate school district. For students with talent, having teachers who have engaged in such teacher exchanges has many advantages. They have the advantage of working with a better-informed teacher. Teachers with insight into the human condition are better able to challenge their students. These teachers are often willing to set up similar experiences when they arrange for their students to participate in exchange programs as well. In situations where actual student travel is not possible due to policy, geography, or the age of the students, partnerships can be developed through the exchange of letters or videotapes. Or exchanges can be sponsored within a school district between classes, schools, or levels. This model has also been used for international exchange.

Serving Talented Students Through:

Minimum   Maximum

Accelerated content

In-depth immersion in topics

Exploration of interests

Figure 5.56
Spotlight On:
Teacher Exchange

LoS Level: NA

Grade Levels: Elementary through high school teachers

For further information consult: Council on International Teacher Exchange at: www.ciee.org/
Teacher Exchange Register at: www.ats.com.au/~hoddo/

 Spotlight On: Tech Trials

Description. For students interested in instructional media, a program that provides Tech Trials encourages participants to extend their understanding of these devices. What used to be limited to the overhead or slide projector has now been vastly extended, as the media used in instruction have significantly grown. Programs such as Tech Trials can provide a base through which students develop their talents in design and application by using these technological devices. At Tech Trials, students can represent their schools in a competition at which they display projects developed on instructional media devices. PowerPoint, a presentation software available as part of Microsoft Office, is one format available to the students. Competitors could develop PowerPoint (www.microsoft.com/office/powerpoint/) presentations about topics of their choice. These may be content specific or community- or interest-based. During the Tech Trials, then, students display the PowerPoint presentations they have developed as part of the competition. Students can be judged on the extent to which their presentations communicate their content. Videotaping is a second format for projects. Students select a topic, write a script, film the script, and edit it for presentation. In a program like Tech Trials, students show their films as part of a film festival. Student films are judged on originality, technical proficiency, and storytelling. One student team, for example, presented a documentary on a favorite coach who had died in a car accident during the school year. Not only did they include footage of the sporting events showing his coaching skill but they also included many contributions he had made to their school as a teacher. The final category for entry can be multimedia. In this category, students design presentations using more than one format. Again, these presentations are judged on the extent to which these presentations communicate the content intended by the developers. For talented students, tech trials provide an opportunity to bring their projects to an audience. In addition to the actual tech trials program, many of these projects may be used at school and district events.

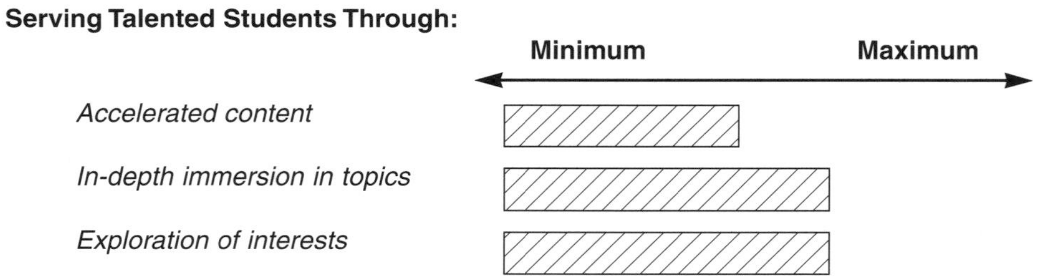

Figure 5.57
Spotlight On:
Tech Trials

Serving Talented Students Through:

Minimum   Maximum

Accelerated content

In-depth immersion in topics

Exploration of interests

LoS Level: 2

Grade Levels: Middle and high school

For further information consult: D. H. Jonassen. (1998). *Learning With Technology: A Constructivist Perspective.* Upper Saddle River, NJ: Prentice Hall.

Spotlight On: Teddy Travels

Description. One way to immerse students in geography, map skills, communication skills, and journaling is to engage in a program such as Teddy Travels. In this program, a teddy bear is sent on an adventure with destinations unknown by collaboration with participants willing to serve as correspondents. The teddies send students postcards or emails describing where they are and the sites they have seen. Students can then locate the sites on the map, keep a journal of their teddy's travels, and write back to Teddy. Some programs are organized by chance, having participants pass Teddy from person to person with the obligation of communicating with the students. In others, teachers direct the travels so that they correspond with the content being covered in their classes. Students look forward to hearing from their teddy and tracing his travels on classroom maps. For students of high ability or talent, this program provides a wealth of information for processing in a written and oral format. Students can write travelogues, compile scrapbooks, predict and plot travel itineraries, correspond with others at Teddy Travels sites, develop Teddy Travels Web sites (e.g., www.ljbear.com and h-files.com), guess the location of Teddy based on his picture at a site, or study the culture of Teddy's destination. The possibilities are endless. Student enthusiasm runs high as they follow their friend on the many adventures (but student-generated Web sites are typically abandoned after the teddy returns). Teachers find volunteers willing to travel with Teddy easy to recruit and enthusiastic about participating in his travels throughout the academic year.

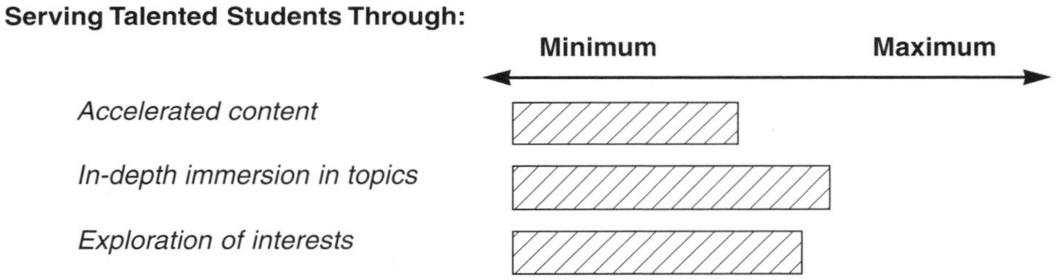

Serving Talented Students Through:

Minimum   Maximum

Accelerated content

In-depth immersion in topics

Exploration of interests

Figure 5.58
Spotlight On:
Teddy Travels

LoS Level: 1

Grade Levels: Elementary to middle school

For further information consult: www.ljbear.com/

  Spotlight On: Video Yearbook

Description. One of the new approaches to assembling yearbooks is to put them on CD-ROM. Beyond the conventional, yearbooks can be converted into video history of student activities across the year. The advantage beyond the typical hardbound form is that videotaping allows students to see events as they unfold rather than see stagnant pictures. When schools make the decision to use video in addition to, or instead of, typical formats, students have new responsibilities to undertake. Identifying activities to be included prior to the event is necessary, as pictures cannot be restaged. Directing the shoot is essential as there is only one opportunity to get the footage that tells the desired story. Assembling the footage into the story of the academic year is vital, as that is the purpose of piece. Talented students find many openings for talent development in either printed or video formats. Planning, content selection, creating the images, editing the content, writing copy, securing advertising support, marketing the products, keeping track of expenditures, working with advisors, and handling incoming sales funds all need to be under control. Matching students to activities that they are interested in is what gives them the opportunity to develop new capabilities or to sharpen those they already have. There are many commercial Web sites and local videographers that are easily accessible when considering compiling a video yearbook. It is essential that advisors remember that this is a student piece and that students should have primary input into the contents and form of the book while under the advisor's supervision. These decisions should not be left to the videographers. It is through the planning and creation of the yearbook that talents are developed. When students are given the opportunity to make as many decisions as possible about the project, talent growth is more likely to occur.

Figure 5.59
Spotlight On:
Video Yearbook

Serving Talented Students Through:

	Minimum	Maximum
Accelerated content	▨	
In-depth immersion in topics	▨▨	
Exploration of interests	▨▨▨	

LoS Level: 2

Grade Levels: Elementary through high school

For further information consult: Your school's yearbook advisors

 Spotlight On: Volunteering

Description. Volunteering is an effective way for students to develop talents. In particular, they can identify areas in which they are interested and further develop that interest through participation. First-hand experience quickly makes it apparent when talent is needed and how extensive that talent must be. The qualities needed to help build a home through Habitat for Humanity will differ from volunteering at a camp for students with disabilities. Taking up a hammer requires different skills from being someone's hands and eyes at camp. A plethora of volunteering opportunities are available in any community. Calling the a local social service agency is a first step that can be taken to identify the volunteering needs in a local community. Schools, churches, and service organizations such as Lions Club and Rotary are sure to have volunteer opportunities available. On a larger scale, volunteer positions can be researched online. Regardless of the tack taken, volunteering is an excellent way to extend talent to those who need it the most in a manner that contributes to the overall well-being of others. Students not only have the chance to further develop their own abilities but they are also given insight into the necessity to do so. In Table 5.10, a few national organizations engaged in volunteering are listed with the Web site address for each.

Organization	URL
Building With Books	www.buildingwithbooks.org
Habitat for Humanity	www.habitat.org
Key Club	www.keyclub.org/flashpage.htm
Kids Care	www.kidscare.org/kidscare/index.htm
Landmark Volunteers	www.volunteers.com
Latitudes International	www.latitudesinternational.com/home.html
United Way	www.unitedway.org/
Visions Service Adventures	www.visions-adventure.org

Table 5.10
Sample Web Sites
for Volunteering

Serving Talented Students Through:

Minimum   Maximum

Accelerated content

In-depth immersion in topics

Exploration of interests

LoS Level: 2

Figure 5.60
Spotlight On:
Volunteering

Grade Levels: Elementary through high school

For further information consult: B. A. Lewis & P. Espeland. (1995). *The Kid's Guide to Service Projects: Over 500 Service Ideas for Young People Who Want to Make a Difference.* Minneapolis, MN: Freespirit Publishing.

 Spotlight On: Windsong Pictures

Description. Windsong Pictures is an innovative cinema project in which many agencies, including the Fort Wayne (IN) Community Schools, collaborate. Under the direction of Michael Floyd, each year the students research, write, produce, film, and distribute cinematic productions, including full-length feature films. Facilities on and off campus are used depending on the project. A film entitled *Pirates in Paradise*, included a cast of approximately 250 actors drawn from the professional ranks, 40 schools, and volunteers. Filming took place in Florida, Michigan, and Indiana, with authentic sites being used. Project students engage in gathering props, sewing costumes, scouting sites, researching content, editing film, and hundreds of additional jobs. They also fully engage in the distribution of the film projects. Their marketing strategies have resulted in the films being viewed in actual movie theaters across five continents: North America, Europe, South American, Australia, and Asia. Windsong Pictures sponsors a film festival each year at which the most current productions are shown, technical seminars are conducted, and students mentor students in the art of filmmaking. This project has obvious benefits in career development but also has extensive impact in other content areas including history, design, technology, mathematics, writing, editing, public relations, strategizing, time management, and language. Floyd was 1997 Indiana Christa McAuliffe Fellow (ideanet.doe.state.in.us/reed/newsr/97May/christa1.html).

Figure 5.61
Spotlight On:
Windsong Pictures

Serving Talented Students Through:

	Minimum	Maximum
Accelerated content		
In-depth immersion in topics		
Exploration of interests		

LoS Level: 2

Grade Levels: Elementary through high school

For further information consult: Mr. Michael Floyd   Windsong Pictures
Elmhurst High School   2402 Lake Ave.
3829 Sand Point Road   Ft. Wayne, IN
Fort Wayne, IN 46809   46805
1-219-425-7510

62   Spotlight On: World Wide Web: Monarch Watch

Description. The World Wide Web has become a wonderful source of online experiences. New sites are popping up each day with exciting opportunities for virtual exploration. A number of sites are dedicated to bringing the world to our homes and schools. Adventure is just a click away. Monarch Watch (monarchwatch.org) is an Internet-based educational program managed through the University of Kansas. The site is designed to give students the opportunity to participate in tracking and reporting on the annual migration of the monarch butterfly. Its purpose is to give students (K-12) a base on which they can develop their skills in science while learning about the monarch butterfly, conservation, and technology. Students work as a tracking network, joining researchers and over 100,000 other students from throughout the United States, Canada, and Mexico. Talented students can find sites through which they can focus their attention and develop their skills of inquiry, communication, and investigation. The 2002 weather events that caused a massive dying off of the Monarchs while in their Mexico habitats resulted in exceptionally compelling content for students to study. Students become actively involved in this annual migration by participating in many different activities. They may monitor the migration online, tag butterflies for yearly tracking of flight patterns, plant gardens to attract the monarchs, and subscribe to the project's journal. No fee is charged. However, educational materials are available for purchase at the Web site. For other online educational opportunities, see Table 5.11.

Serving Talented Students Through:

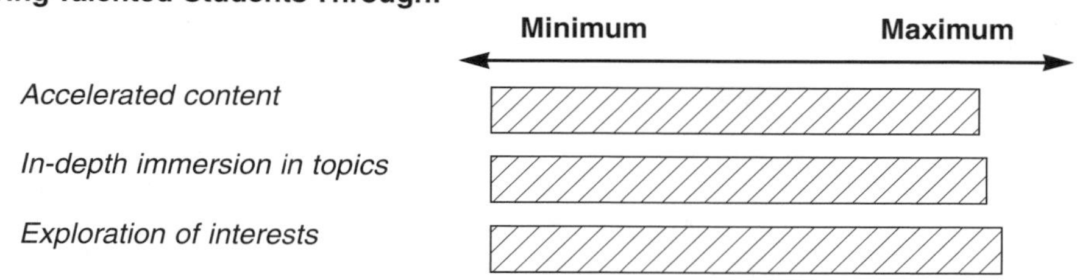

Figure 5.62
Spotlight On:
World Wide Web

	Minimum	Maximum
Accelerated content	//////////////////////////	
In-depth immersion in topics	//////////////////////////	
Exploration of interests	//////////////////////////	

LoS Level: 1

Grade Levels: Elementary through high school

Web Site	URL
Alaskan Dog Sled Racing	www.iditarod.com
Discovery Television Network	www.discovery.com
Egyptian Mathematics	www.ibiscom.com
Eyewitness History	www.eyelid.co.uk.htm
NASA's Moon Link Project	www.moonlink.com

Table 5.11
Sample Web Sites for
Online Education
Opportunities

 63   **Spotlight On: Writer's Forum**

Description. The idea of a writer's forum is to give youths an opportunity to share their work for critical analysis and evaluation. Writers talking to writers give the participants feedback from the people they most highly value—other writers. A writer's forum can be established in a class, school, district or Internet site. Threaded discussion and other communication sites are available commercially and through many school district sites. One Web site reports on teaching writing on the Internet (www.4teachers. org/feature/nebraska-yaf/index.shtml).

Many believe the geographic distance between authors and reviewers provides anonymity for both parties and results in the honest communication that leads to skill development. The forum can encourage students to produce more text and their reviewers to comment more honestly. Each piece of writing is considered for its own merit without regard to author status: economic, social, or academic. There are more strategies available each day for students to engage in writing activities. It is through Writer's Forum structures that they can garner the criticism that professional writers use to develop their craft. The more they mirror the activities of the professional, the more they will augment their own talents. Discussion programs are available through Internet sites listed in Table 5.12.

Table 5.12
Sample Discussion
Sites

Discussion Sites	URL
Blackboard	www.blackboard.com
Ceilidh	www.lilikoi.com
E-Mind	www.emind.com
Global Knowledge	www.globalknowledge.com

Figure 5.63
Spotlight On:
Writer's Forum

Serving Talented Students Through:

Minimum   Maximum

Accelerated content

In-depth immersion in topics

Exploration of interests

LoS Level: 3
Grade Levels: Elementary through high school

For further information consult: www.cityslidecom to develop your own discussion forum.

Spotlight On: Young Authors

Description. Young-authors programs are designed to give students an opportunity to experience the joys of writing and producing original books. These programs take many forms and adapt easily to the goals and constraints of any particular school district. Typically, young-authors programs are structured in one of two ways. Some hold young-authors events during the course of a school year. Other schools make the program ongoing, and students meet as a regular part of their writing and reading curricula. Regardless of the structure, the purposes are the same. They are to encourage students to write and enjoy reading. In most schools, all students are eligible to participate. They need only to produce a book for others to read. Generally, guidelines are given to the students, including specifications for length, illustrations, format, story elements, and entry categories. Some schools combine the writing experience with other activities, such as inviting professional authors to speak to the students; publishing student books on the Internet; visiting local libraries that invite celebrity readers; and staging classroom read-ins, young-authors exhibitions, and competitions. Young authors can be conducted as an after-school program, optional enrichment assignment, in-class activity, or full-time class. Sponsors for programs are generally the local school districts, reading advocacy associations, and teachers. However, libraries, service and parent organizations, high school clubs, or individuals can initiate a young-authors program. Neighborhood parents can easily join together and make young authors an exciting summer activity for their children. Ask the local library to set aside a table to display the children's work!

Serving Talented Students Through:

Figure 5.64
Spotlight On:
Young Authors

	Minimum	Maximum

Accelerated content

In-depth immersion in topics

Exploration of interests

LoS Level: 1/2/3 (depending on program organization)

Grade Levels: Elementary and middle school

For further information consult: Your school librarian or reading teacher. Many Web sites are available.

 65   Spotlight On: Zoo Apprenticeships

Description. Apprenticeships are an exciting way for talented students to develop their capabilities. The zoo is a great place to be working. Some zoos offer apprenticeships to youth of all ages. These positions typically require formal application and review of applicants' skills and motivation. For those selected, an incredible experience follows. For some zoos, apprenticeships are available only in the summer. Other zoos have apprenticeships all year long. The responsibilities of the apprentices vary. In general, apprentices can expect to be involved in the feeding and care of the animals, maintenance of zoo and animal facilities, visitor services, or veterinary activities. For students considering veterinary or service careers, apprenticing at the zoo gives valuable insight into such work. Students of all ages can find apprenticeship opportunities. They are most plentiful, however, for students 16 and older. Through the apprentice experience, people can work in real-life circumstances with actual performance responsibilities. There is no better way to evaluate a zoo career path. Apprenticeships are available in numerous disciplines and are a teaching strategy of choice for skill development This model is also used in other career areas under the name *practicum* or *internship*. Citizen School, a program based in Massachusetts, describes their apprentice programs as follows:

> In our hands-on apprenticeships, our volunteer Citizen Teachers work with small groups of young apprentices on a huge range of practical, satisfying, real-life projects—from making a quilt to fixing a computer, from running a business to writing a children's book. Apprentices come away with a deep understanding of the subject, a sense of "real world" expertise, and a high-quality product or performance that has value to the community. Our law apprenticeships, for example, end in mock trials held at Boston's new Federal Court House, in front of real federal judges! (www.volunteersolutions.org)

Figure 5.65
Spotlight On:
Zoo Apprenticeships

Serving Talented Students Through:

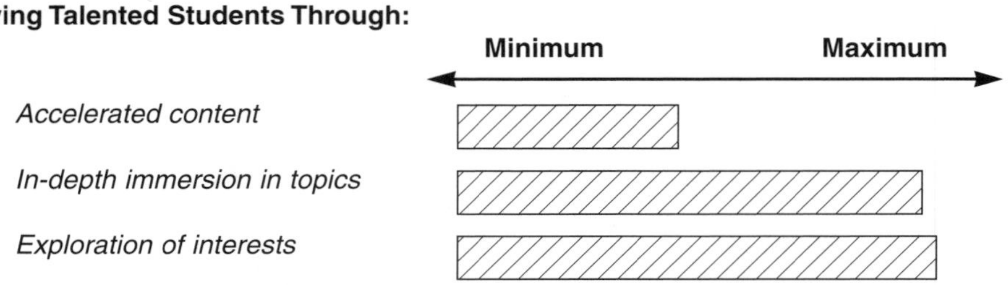

	Minimum	Maximum
Accelerated content		
In-depth immersion in topics		
Exploration of interests		

LoS Level: 3

Grade Levels: Elementary through high school

For further information consult: www.nait.ab.ca/apprenticeship/info.htm

Resource A: PreK–12 Gifted Program Standards (National Association for Gifted Children)

STANDARD 1: CURRICULUM AND INSTRUCTION ■

1.1 Differentiated curriculum for the gifted learner must span grades preK–12.

1.2 Regular classroom curricula and instruction must be adapted, modified, or replaced to meet the unique needs of gifted learners.

1.3 Instructional pace must be flexible to allow for the accelerated learning of gifted learners as appropriate.

1.4 Educational opportunities for subject and grade skipping must be provided to gifted learners.

1.5 Learning opportunities for gifted learners must consist of a continuum of differentiated curricular options, instructional approaches, and resource materials.

■ STANDARD 2: PROGRAM ADMINISTRATION AND MANAGEMENT

2.1 Appropriately qualified personnel must direct services for the education of gifted learners.

2.2 Gifted education programming must be integrated into the general education program.

2.3 Gifted education programming must include positive working relationships with constituency and advocacy groups, as well as compliance agencies.

2.4 Requisite resources and materials must be provided to support the efforts of gifted education programming.

■ STANDARD 3: PROGRAM DESIGN

3.1 Rather than any single gifted program, a continuum of programming services must exist for gifted learners.

3.2 Gifted education must be adequately funded.

3.3 Gifted education programming must evolve from a comprehensive and sound base.

3.4 Gifted education programming services must be an integral part of the general education school day.

3.5 Flexible groupings of students must be developed in order to facilitate differentiated instruction and curriculum.

■ STANDARD 4: PROGRAM EVALUATION

4.1 An evaluation must be purposeful.

4.2 An evaluation must be efficient and economic.

4.3 An evaluation must be conducted competently and ethically.

4.4 The evaluation results must be made available through a written report.

■ STANDARD 5: SOCIO-EMOTIONAL GUIDANCE AND COUNSELING

5.1 Gifted learners must be provided with differentiated guidance efforts to meet their unique socio-emotional development.

5.2 Gifted learners must be provided with career guidance services especially designed for their unique needs.

5.3 Gifted at-risk students must be provided with guidance and counseling to help them reach their potential.

5.4 Gifted learners must be provided with effective curriculum in addition to differentiated guidance and counseling services.

5.5 Underachieving gifted learners must be served rather than omitted from differentiated services.

STANDARD 6: ■
PROFESSIONAL DEVELOPMENT

6.1 A comprehensive staff development program must be provided for all school staff involved in the education of gifted learners.

6.2 Only qualified personnel should be involved in the education of gifted learners.

6.3 School personnel require support for their specific efforts related to the education of gifted learners.

6.4 The educational staff must be provided with time and other support for the preparation and development of the differentiated education plans, materials, and curriculum.

STANDARD 7: STUDENT IDENTIFICATION ■

7.1 A comprehensive and cohesive process for student nomination must be coordinated in order to determine eligibility for gifted education services.

7.2 Instruments used for student assessment to determine eligibility for gifted education services must measure diverse abilities, talents, strengths, and needs in order to provide students an opportunity to demonstrate any strengths.

7.3 A student assessment profile of individual strengths and needs must be developed to plan appropriate intervention.

7.4 All student identification procedures and instruments must be based on current theory and research.

7.5 Written procedures for student identification must include at the very least provisions for informed consent, student retention, student reassessment, student exiting, and appeals procedures.

Resource B: Standards for Programs Including the Gifted and Talented (The Association for Gifted)

■ **STANDARD 1. PROGRAM DESIGN**

1.1 Programs for the gifted and talented are articulated with general education programs.

1.2 Programs are comprehensive, structured, and sequenced across grade levels.

1.3 Programs are an integral part of the school day and may be extended to other school and community related settings.

1.4 Administrative structures and program options are based on student needs.

1.5 All gifted and talented students are assured programs commensurate with their abilities.

1.6 Resources for program development and implementation are distributed equitably throughout the school district.

1.7 Programs incorporate a blend of community resources and school-based support services in program development and delivery.

1.8 Specialists in gifted child education are consulted in program policy development.

1.9 Ongoing program evaluation activities are conducted for the purpose of continued program development.

STANDARD 2. PROFESSIONAL DEVELOPMENT ■

2.1 Coursework for initial teacher preparation includes systematic instruction in the nature and needs of gifted and talented students.

2.2 Educators providing direct service to gifted and talented students have completed the following: an undergraduate emphasis in liberal arts or a content area; professional coursework in general teacher education and/or content area; teaching experience; specialized training in gifted child education in accordance with CEC/NCATE guidelines for teacher education majors, or demonstrated knowledge of the nature and needs of gifted and talented students for content specialists.

2.3 Noncertified individuals who offer specialized instruction or mentoring for gifted and talented students demonstrate understanding of the nature and needs of these students.

2.4 Educators specializing in gifted child education demonstrate mastery of this area in accordance with CEC/NCATE standards for personnel preparation and sufficient knowledge of the content area(s) they instruct to provide effective differentiated instruction to gifted and talented students.

2.5 Educators specializing in content areas demonstrate mastery of the content area(s) they instruct to provide effective differentiated instruction to these students.

2.6 Educators with administrative or instructional responsibility for programs including gifted and talented students implement plans for their own continuing professional development.

2.7 Professional development opportunities in gifted child education are available on a regular basis to all staff members.

STANDARD 3. ASSESSMENT ■
FOR IDENTIFICATION

3.1 Instruments and procedures used for identifying students measure diverse abilities and intelligences.

3.2 Assessments for identification purposes include information on the students' potential and demonstrated abilities.

3.3 Instruments and procedures used in the identification process correspond to the area(s) of ability being assessed.

3.4 Data collection procedures employ qualitative and quantitative formats.

3.5 Nondiscriminatory assessment procedures and instruments are used in order to ensure that special populations are fairly assessed.

3.6 The identification process is open and available to all students.

3.7 Systems are established through which assessment data can be shared with parents, educational staff members, and students in ways that are meaningful and useful for each group's varied purposes.

3.8 Trained personnel are used at the different stages of the assessment process according to their expertise in the various aspects of assessment.

3.9 A systematic and ongoing plan to review and reevaluate current assessment procedures is employed.

■ STANDARD 4. CURRICULUM DESIGN

4.1 Curriculum (preschool-12) is articulated, comprehensive, and includes substantive scope and sequence.

4.2 Curriculum is based on the assessed needs of students including the areas of intellectual, emotional, physical, ethical, and social development.

4.3 Curriculum matches substantive content with the developmental levels of the gifted and talented student.

4.4 Curriculum incorporates content and experiences that employ and facilitate understanding of the latest ideas, principles, and technology in a given content area.

4.5 Curriculum provides differentiation and challenges for students through involvement with advanced and rigorous content and procedures.

4.6 Students develop critical and creative thinking skills through instruction and experiences rooted in the content areas.

4.7 Students have opportunities to engage in experiential and interactive learning involving real life experiences that may result in the development of sophisticated products.

4.8 Flexible pacing is employed, allowing students to learn at the pace and level appropriate to their abilities and skills.

4.9 Curriculum addresses the attitudes and skills needed for lifelong independent learning.

4.10 Specialists in content areas instructional techniques and gifted child education work with curriculum planners when curriculum is being planned and evaluated.

SOURCE: Adapted from The Association for Gifted. (1989). Used with permission.

Resource C: Spotlight Programs: Relationships to Standards and LoS Level

NATIONAL ASSOCIATION FOR GIFTED CHILDREN (NAGC) AND THE ASSOCIATION FOR GIFTED (TAG) STANDARDS AND LEVEL OF SERVICE (LOS)

Spotlight Program	NAGC Standard	TAG Standard	LoS
1. 4-H	1.3, 1.5, 2.4	1.7, 4.4, 4.6, 4.7	2
2. Academic Competitions	1.3, 1.5, 2.4	1.7, 4.4, 4.5, 4.9	3
3. Accelerated Readers	1.2, 1.3, 1.5, 2.4	4.4, 4.8	1
4. Archaeological Digs	1.2, 1.3	4.5, 4.6, 4.7	1
5. Ask an Engineer	1.2, 5.2	4.3, 4.4, 4.5	1
6. Block Scheduling	1.3, 3.5	1.4, 4.8	1
7. Coteaching	6.1, 6.4	2.6, 2.7	1
8. Dual Enrollment	1.3, 1.4, 3.5, 3.6, 5.2	1.7, 4.4, 4.5, 4.6, 4.8	4

9. Community Service	1.2, 1.3, 1.5, 2.4	1.7, 4.7, 4.9	1
10. Computer Tech	1.2, 5.2	4.4, 4.6, 4.7	1
11. Debate/Forensics	1.3, 1.5	4.5, 4.6	3
12. Distance Learning	1.2, 1.3, 1.4, 1.5	1.7, 4.4, 4.5, 4.8, 4.9	2
13. Dress-Up Box	2.4	1.7, 4.3	1
14. Dual-Language Instruction	1.2, 1.5	4.3, 4.5, 4.6	2
15. E-Pals	1.2	4.4, 4.7	1
16. Family Excursions	2.4	1.7, 4.3	1
17. Family Investigations	1.5	4.4, 4.5, 4.6	1
18. Field Trips	1.2	1.7, 4.4	1
19. Flex Classes	1.2, 1.3, 1.4, 1.5	4.5	4
20. Foreign Exchange	1.2, 1.5	4.4, 4.6, 4.7, 4.9	3
21. Girls/Boys State	1.3, 1.5, 2.4	1.7, 4.5, 4.6, 4.7	3
22. History Fair	1.2, 1.3, 1.5	4.5, 4.6, 4.7, 4.9	2
23. Intramural Sports	1.3, 3.5	4.2, 4.9	1
24. Inventions	1.2, 1.3, 1.5	4.4, 4.5, 4.6, 4.7, 4.8, 4.9	2
25. Jazz Band	1.3, 1.5	4.6, 4.7, 4.9	3
26. Junior Achievement	2.4, 5.2	1.7, 4.4, 4.6, 4.7, 4.9	2
27. Junior Great Books	1.2, 1.3, 1.5	1.7, 4.5, 4.9	2,3
28. LEGO League	1.3, 1.5, 3.4	1.7, 4.4, 4.5, 4.6, 4.7, 4.9	2,3
29. Mental Math	1.2, 1.3, 1.5	4.5, 4.6	3
30. Mentorships	1.3, 1.5, 2.4, 5.2	1.7, 4.4, 4.5, 4.7, 4.9	3
31. Model United Nations	1.3, 1.5, 2.4	1.7, 4.5, 4.6, 4.7	3
32. Opening Night	1.3, 1.5	4.6, 4.7	2
33. Original Research	1.2, 1.3, 1.5	4.4, 4.5, 4.6, 4.7, 4.8, 4.9	2,3,4
34. Outdoors Education	1.2, 1.3, 1.5	1.7, 4.6	2
35. Parenting Class	2.3, 7.1	2.3	NA
36. Peer Mediation	5.3, 5.4	4.6, 4.7	2
37. Power of the Pen	1.5, 3.2	4.3, 4.6, 4.7	2
38. Problem-Based Learning	1.2, 1.5, 3.5	4.3-4.9	1
39. Professional Development	2.1, 6.1, 6.2	2.4, 2.5, 2.6, 2.7	NA
40. Quiz Bowl	1.3, 1.5	1.7, 4.5	3
41. Reenactments	1.2, 1.3, 1.5	4.5, 4.6, 4.7, 4.9	1
42. Science Fair	1.2, 1.3, 1.5	1.7, 4.4, 4.5, 4.6, 4.7, 4.8	2,3,4

43. Scouts	5.3	4.7, 4.9	2
44. Seminars	1.3, 1.5, 3.5, 5.1	4.4, 4.5, 4.6, 4.7, 4.8, 4.9	3
45. Show Choir	1.3, 1.5	4.5, 4.7	3
46. Space Camp	1.3, 1.5	4.3-4.7	2
47. Speakers Bureau	1.2, 1.3, 1.5, 2.4	1.7, 4.7, 4.9	3
48. Special Olympics	1.5	4.6, 4.7, 4.9	2
49. Sports Day	1.3, 1.5	4.7, 4.9	1
50. Student Council	1.3, 1.5	4.5, 4.7, 4.9	2
51. Student Newspaper	1.3, 1.5	4.5, 4.6, 4.7	2
52. Summer Stars	1.3, 1,5	4.4	2,3
53. Sustained Silent Reading	1.3, 3.2	4.8	1
54. Talent Shows	1.3, 1.5	4.6, 4.7	2
55. Tarheel Museum	1.3, 1.5	4.6, 4.7	1,3
56. Teacher Exchange	6.4	2.6, 2.7	NA
57. Tech Trials	1.2, 1.3	4.4, 4.7	2
58. Teddy Travels	1.2, 1.5	4.7	1
59. Video Yearbook	1.3, 1.5	4.4, 4.6, 4.7	2
60. Volunteering	1.3, 1.5, 2.4 5.2	1.7, 4.7, 4.9	2
61. Windsong Pictures	1.3, 1.5	1.7, 4.4, 4.5, 4.6, 4.7, 4.8	2
62. World Wide Web	2.4	4.4, 4.5, 4.6, 4.7, 4.9	1
63. Writers Forum	1.2, 1.3, 1.5	4.6, 4.7, 4.8, 4.9	3
64. Young Authors	1.2, 1.3, 1.5	1.7, 4.6, 4.7, 4.8, 4.9	1,2,3
65. Zoo Apprenticeships	1.3, 1.5, 2.4, 5.2	1.7, 4.4, 4.6, 4.7, 4.8, 4.9	3

NA = Not Applicable

SOURCE: Adapted from National Association for Gifted Children (1998) and The Association for Gifted (1989). Used with permission. See also Parke, 1991.

Resource D:
Sample Forms

Profile of Ability

Name: _____   School: _____

Address: _____   Grade: _____   Date of Birth:_____

Parent Name: _____   Phone: _____

Completion Date: _____

Assessment Data*:

Test/Assessment	Score	Date

Placement Decisions:

Effective Date:

Evaluation Data:

Effective Date:

Signatures:

*Norm-referenced tests, criterion-referenced tests, inventories, products, competitions, nominations. Please write anecdotal information on back of page.

Interest Inventory

Name:_____   Teacher: _____

Grade: _____   School: _____   Date:_____

1. What is your favorite subject in school? What is your least-favorite subject?

2. What are your two favorite books?

3. What activities do you most like to do on the weekends?

4. When you study, on which subject do you start? Why?

5. If you could invite a famous person to dinner, whom would you invite? Why?

6. What do you wonder about?

7. Would you rather read directions for building a model airplane or have them   explained to you?

8. If you could choose a project to develop for fun, what would it be?

Hidden Programs Rating Chart					
Program Title:					
	Rating*				
Factor	**1**	**2**	**3**	**4**	**5**
1. Students are active learners.					
2. Students are involved in decision making.					
3. Students learn strategies for how to learn.					
4. Teachers facilitate learning.					
5. Cooperative and collaborative skills are developed.					
6. Interdisciplinary focus is part of the curricular design.					
7. Materials and resources are rich and far-reaching.					
8. Products have real-world applications.					
9. Multiple outlets for products are used.					
10. Instructional process includes parents and community members.					
Total Points					

Rating Scale*

1 = Very little evidence
2 = Little evidence
3 = Somewhat evident
4 = Very evident
5 = Extremely evident

Comments:

Seminar in Discovery Application

Name: _____

Grade: _____   Term of Study: _____

Homeroom Teacher: _____   Seminar Sponsor: _____

I am submitting this application for evaluation and possible acceptance into the *Seminar in Discovery Program*. I understand that if accepted, I will attend this seminar for one semester in lieu of the class.

During the course of the term I intend to do the following:

I expect to use the following resources:

As a culminating project/event, I intend to:

Student Signature: _____   Date: _____

I, _____, agree to serve as the sponsor for
this student. I agree to provide the following resources (time & materials):

_____

_____

Decision: [_____]   **See comments on other side** ⟶

Independent Study Proposal

Name: _____   Supervisor: _____

Start Date: _____   End Date: _____

I would like to find out more about:

Circle the idea you like best.

These are three questions I have about my topic:

Circle the questions you will answer

These are the materials I may need:

This is my basic plan:

Topic:

Question:

Completion Date:

I can tell others about my topic by:

Circle the idea you will use.

I will know I did a good job by:

Circle the idea you will use.

Independent Study Proposal

Name: _____

Grade: _____   Beginning Date: _____

Homeroom Teacher: _____   Completion Date: _____

Questions I want to answer:

    1.

    2.

    3.

Resources I will use:

    1.

    2.

    3.

Projected Activities & Timeline:

    1.

    2.

    3.

Reporting options:

    1.

    2.

Evaluation options:

    1.

    2.

Highlight chosen options.

Student Signature: _____

Sponsoring Teacher Signature: _____

| **Accepted   Revise   Rejected** | | ***See Comments on Back of Sheet*** |

Personal Field Trip Application
Name: _____
Home Room: _____ Home Phone: _____
Destination: Purpose: Resulting Product: Trip Date: Classes/Activities Missed: Approvals/Arrangements needed:
Student Signature: _____ Parent Signature: _____ Sponsoring Teacher Signature: _____
Liability Form on File: _____ Date: _____ Approval [_____] By: _____ Date: _____

References

Achter, J. A., Benbow, C. P., & Lubinski, D. (1997). Rethinking multipotentiality among the intellectually gifted: A critical review and recommendations. *Roeper Review, 41*(1), 5-13.

Association for Gifted, The. (1989*). Standards for programs involving gifted and talented students.* Reston, VA: Council for Exceptional Children.

Bany-Winers, L. (1997). *Theater games and activities for kids.* Chicago: Chicago Review Press.

Barnett, L. B., & Darden, W. G. (1993). Education patterns of academically talented youth. *Roeper Review, 37*(4), 161-168.

Bellanca, J. (1998). Teaching for intelligence. *Phi Delta Kappan, 79*(9), 658-661.

Betts, G. T. (1995). Encouraging lifelong learning through the autonomous learner model. In J. Genshaft, M. Bireley, & C. Hollinger, (Eds.), *Serving gifted and talented students: A resource for school personnel* (pp. 135-154). Austin, TX: Pro-Ed.

Bloom, B. (1956). *Taxonomy of educational objectives: The classification of educational goals. Handbook I: Cognitive domain.* New York: Longman, Greens.

Bloom, B. (1985). *Developing talent in young people.* New York: Ballantine.

Brown, M. K., Chou, L., Goldberg, N., & Moretti, F. (1991*). Archaeotype: Discovering the past through simulated archaeology.* New York: New Lab for Teaching and Learning.

Burns, D. (2002). Standards and curriculum development. *Education Update, 44*(1), 3.

Burz, H., & Marshall, K. (1999). *Performance-based curriculum for music and the visual arts: From knowing to showing.* Thousand Oaks, CA: Corwin.

Byl, J. (2002). *Intramural recreation: A step-by-step guide to creating an effective program.* Champaign, IL: Human Kinetics.

Canciamilla, L. S. (1999). Align your system for success. *Thrust for Educational Leadership, 28*(3), 14-17.

Cantrelle, M. L., & Edbon, S. A. (1997). The Summer Stars program. *Educational Leadership, 55*(1), 38-42.

Carle, E. (2000). *Does a kangaroo have a mother, too?* New York: Harper Collins.

Cavarretta, J. (1998). Parents are a school's best friend. *Educational Leadership, 55*(8), 12-16.

Chalker, C. S. (1996). *Effective alternative education programs: Best practices from planning through evaluation.* Lancaster, PA: Technomic Publishing.

Clark, G., & Zimmerman, E. (1998). Nurturing the arts in programs for gifted and talented students. *Phi Delta Kappan, 79*(10), 747-749.

Clifford, M. M. (1990). Students need challenge, not easy success. *Educational Leadership, 48*(1), 22-27.

Cline, S., & Schwartz, D. (1999). *Diverse populations of gifted children: Meeting their needs in the regular classroom and beyond.* Upper Saddle River, NJ: Merrill.

Cooper, C. R. (1998). For the good of humankind: Matching the budding talent with a curriculum conscience. *Gifted Child Quarterly, 42*(4), 238-244.

Cox, J., Daniel, N., & Boston, B. (1985). *Educating able learners.* Austin: University of Texas Press.

Crosby, D., & Britt, L. (1999). *Create your own class newspaper: A complete guide for planning, writing, and publishing a newspaper.* Nashville, TN: Incentive Publications.

Dettmer, P. (1990). *Staff development for gifted programs: Putting it together and making it work.* Washington, DC: Service Publications.

Duper, L. (1996). *160 ways to help the world: Community service projects for young people.* New York: Facts on File.

Edmonds, R. (1979, October). Effective schools for the urban poor. *Educational Leadership,* pp. 15-24.

Feldhusen, J. F. (1994). A case for developing America's talent: How we went wrong and where we go now. *Roeper Review, 16*(4), 231-234.

Feldhusen, J. F. (1995). Talent development: The new direction in gifted education. *Roeper Review, 18*(2), 92-93.

Feldhusen, J. F. (1996). How to identify and develop special talents. *Educational Leadership, 53*(5), 66-70.

Feldhusen, J. F. (1998). Programs for the gifted few or talent development for the many? *Phi Delta Kappan, 79*(10), 735-738.

Feldman, D. H. (1986). *Nature's gambit.* New York: Teacher's College Press.

Feldman, D. H. (2000). Was Mozart at risk? A developmentalist looks at extreme talent. In R. C. Friedman & B. M. Shore (Eds.), *Talents unfolding* (pp. 251-263). Washington, DC: American Psychological Association.

Ferrari, M., Taylor, R., Vanlehn, K. (1999). Adapting work simulations for schools. *Journal of Educational Computing Research, 21*(1), 25-53.

Fogarty, R. (1995). *Best practices for the learner-centered classroom.* Arlington Heights, IL: IRI/SkyLight Training and Publishing.

Freedman, E., & Montgomery, J. F. (1994). Parent education and student achievement. *Thrust for educational leadership, 24*(3), 40-45.

Fulkerson, J. L. (1995). A talent approach to district programming for gifted and talented youth K-12. *Roeper Review, 18*(2), 117-121.

Fulkerson, J. L., & Horvich, M. (1998). Talent development: Two perspectives. *Phi Delta Kappan, 79*(10), 756-760.

Gagne, F. (1995). From giftedness to talent: A developmental model and its impact on the language of the field. *Roeper Review, 18*(2), 103-112.

Gallagher, J. J. (1991). Editorial: The gifted: A term with surplus meaning. *Journal for the Education of the Gifted, 14*(4), 353-365.

Gallagher, J. J., & Coleman, M. R. (1995). Perceptions of educational reform by educators representing middle schools, cooperative learning, and gifted education. *Gifted Child Quarterly, (39)*2, 68-76.

Gallagher, J. J., & Sapon-Shevin, M. (1997). Should public schools devote more resources to special programs for gifted students? *CQ Researcher, 7*(12), 281.

Gardner, H. (1983). *Frames of mind: The theory of multiple intelligences.* New York: Basic Books.

Gardner, H. (1997). *Extraordinary minds.* New York: Basic Books.

Gardner, H. (1999). *Intelligence reframed: Multiple intelligences for the 21st century.* New York: Basic Books.

Genshaft, J., Birerley, M., & Hollinger, C. (Eds.), *Serving gifted and talented students: A resource for school personnel.* Austin, TX: Pro-Ed.

Greene, R. (2000). *The teenager's guide to school outside the box.* Mansfield Center, CT: Creative Learning Press.

Gritton, P. (1999). *Encores for choirs: 24 show-stopping concert pieces.* New York: Oxford University Press.

Grote, D., & Zapel, A. (Eds.) (1998). *Play directing in the school: A drama director's survival guide.* Colorado Springs, CO: Meriwether Publishing.

Hansel, B. (1993). *The exchange student's survival kit.* Yarmouth, ME: Intercultural Press.

Haroutounian, J. (1998). Drop the hurdles and open the doors: Fostering talent development through school and community collaboration. *Arts Education Policy Review, 99*(6), 15-25.

Hickey, M. G. (1998). *Bringing history home: Local and family history projects Grades K-6*. Boston: Allyn & Bacon.

House, G. (2002). Lessons from the maze. *Education Update, 44*(1), 1-2.

Howard, M. B. (1993). Service learning: Character education applied. *Educational Leadership, 51*(3), 42-44.

Hughes, C. E., & Murawski, W. A. (2001). Lessons from another field: Applying co-teaching strategies to gifted education. *Gifted Child Quarterly, 45*(3), 195-204.

Isenberg, J. P., & Jalongo, M. R. (2001). *Creative expression and play in early childhood* (3rd ed.). Upper Saddle River, NJ: Prentice Hall.

Johnson, D. W., & Johnson, R. T. (1992). What to say to advocates for the gifted. *Educational Leadership, 50*(2), 44-48.

Jolles, R. L. (2000). *How to run presentations and workshops*. New York: John Wiley.

Jonassen, D. H. (1998). *Learning with technology: A constructivist perspective*. Upper Saddle River, NJ: Prentice Hall.

Joyce, B. R. (1991). Common misconceptions about cooperative learning and gifted students. *Educational Leadership, 48*(6), 72-75.

Karnes, F. A., & Riley, T. L. (1997). Enhancing reading and writing through competitions. *Reading Teacher, 51*(3), 270-272.

Kennedy, M. (2002). *Special Olympics*. New York: Children's Books.

Kerr, B. A., & Colangelo, N. (1988). The college plans of academically talented students. *Journal of Counseling and Development, 67*(1), 42-48.

Lewis, B. A., (1996). Serving others hooks gifted students on learning. *Educational Leadership, 53*(5), 70-75.

Lewis, B. A., & Espeland, P. (1995). *The kid's guide to service projects: Over 500 service ideas for young people who want to make a difference*. Minneapolis, MN: Freespirit Publishing.

Loomis, C., & Paul, C. (2001). *Fodor's family adventures: More than 700 great trips for you and your kids of all ages*. New York: Fodor's Travel Publications.

Lumsdea, K., & Jones, S. (1996). *Ready-to-use secondary P. E. activities program: Lessons, tournaments and assessments for grades 6-12*. Upper Saddle River, NJ: Prentice Hall.

Marek-Schroer, M. F., & Schroer, N. A. (1993). Identifying and providing for musically gifted young children. *Roeper Review, 16*(1), 33-37.

McKinnon, D. H., & Nolan, C. J. (1999). Distance education for the gifted and talented: An interactive design model. *Roeper Review, 12*(4), 320-325.

Miller, M. A., & McCartan, A. (1990). Making the case for new interdisciplinary programs. *Change, 22*(3), 28-36.

Murphy, P., Klages, E., & Shore, L. (1996). *The science explorer: Family experiments from the world's favorite hands-on science museum*. New York: Henry Holt.

National Association for Gifted Children. (1998). *Pre-K–Grade 12 gifted program standards*. Washington, DC: National Association for Gifted Children.

Nottage, C., & Morse, M. (2000). *IIM: Independent investigation method teacher manual (K-12)*. Epping, NH: Active Learning Systems.

Olszewski-Kubilius, P., & Limburg-Weber, L. (1999). Options for middle school and secondary level gifted students. *Journal of Secondary Gifted Education, 11*(1), 4-10.

Owen, L. B., & Lamb, C. E. (1996). *Bringing the NCTM standards to life: Best practices from elementary educators*. Princeton Junction, NJ: Eye on Education.

Parke, B. N. (1983). Use of self-instructional materials with gifted primary-aged students. *Gifted Child Quarterly, 27*(1), 29-34.

Parke, B. N. (1989). *Gifted students in regular classrooms*. Boston: Allyn & Bacon.

Parke, B. N. (1991). Proposed NCATE guidelines for gifted child education. *Journal for the Education of the Gifted, 14*(4), 423-426.

Parke, B. N. (1995). Developing curricular interventions for the gifted. In J. L. Genshaft, M. Bierely, & C. L. Hollinger (Eds.), *Serving gifted and talented students: A resource for school personnel* (pp. 123-134). Austin, TX: Pro-Ed.

Parke, B. N., & Byrnes, P. (1984). Toward objectifying the measurement of creativity. *Roeper Review, 6*(4), 216-218.

Parke, B., Nichols, J., & Brown, A. (2002). Collegiate Connection: A program to encourage the success of student participation in high school/university dual enrollment. *Midwest Educational Researcher, 15*(2), 23-31.

Parker, D. (2001). *Roadmap to confident basic public speaking* (2nd ed.). Philadelphia: Xlibris.

Parnes, S. (1977). Guiding creative action. *Gifted Child Quarterly, 21*(4), 460-472.

Passe, J., & Whitley, I. (1998). The *best* museum for kids? The one they build themselves! *Social Studies, 89*(4), 183-187.

Peterson's Guides (Ed.). (2002). *Peterson's guide to distance learning programs* (2nd ed.). Trenton, NJ: Thompson Learning.

Piirto, J. (1999). *Talented children and adults: Their development and education.* New York: Merrill.

Reilly, J. (1992). *Mentorship.* Mansfield Center, CT: Creative Learning Press.

Renzulli, J. S. (1977). *The enrichment triad model: A guide for developing defensible programs for the gifted and talented.* Mansfield Center, CT: Creative Learning Press.

Renzulli, J. S. (1994a). *Schools for talent development.* Mansfield Center, CT: Creative Learning Press.

Renzulli, J. S. (1994b). Teachers as talent scouts. *Educational Leadership, 52*(4), 75-82.

Renzulli, J. S. (1998). A rising tide lifts all ships. *Phi Delta Kappan, 80*(2), 104-112.

Renzulli, J. S., & Reis, S. (1997). Giftedness in middle school students: A talent development perspective. In P. S. George, J. S. Renzulli, & S. M. Reis (Eds.), *Dilemmas in talent development in the middle grades: Two views.* Columbus, OH: National Middle School Association.

Renzulli, J. S., Reis, S., & Smith, L. H. (1981). The revolving door identification model. Mansfield Center, CT: Creative Learning Press.

Renzulli, J. S., & Smith, L. H. (1979). A guidebook for developing *individualized educational programs for gifted and talented students.* Mansfield Center, CT: Creative Learning Press.

Renzulli, J. S., Smith, L. H., & Reis, S. M. (1982). Curriculum compacting: An essential strategy for working with gifted students. *The Elementary School Journal, 82,* 185-194.

Rhem, J. (1998). Problem-based learning. Retrieved September 1, 2002, from www.ntlf.com/html/pi/9812/pbl_1

Rimm, S. (2001). *Keys to parenting the gifted child.* Hauppauge, NY: Barron's Educational Series.

Robbins, P., Gregory, G., & Herndon, L. (2000). *Thinking inside the block schedule: Strategies for teaching in extended periods of time.* Thousand Oaks, CA: Corwin.

Robinson, N. M. (2000). Giftedness in very young children: How seriously should it be taken? In R. C. Jenkins & B. M. Shore (Eds.), *Talents unfolding* (pp. 7-26). Washington, DC: American Psychological Association.

Rogers, K. B. (1992). Acceleration: What we do vs. what we know. *Educational Leadership, 50*(2), 58-62.

Roth, S. F. (1998*). Past into present: Effective techniques for first-person historical interpretation.* Chapel Hill: University of North Carolina Press.

Runco, M. A., & Nemiro, J. (1994). Problem finding, creativity, and giftedness. *Roeper Review, 16*(4), 235-242.

Sapon-Shevin, M. (1994). Why gifted students belong in inclusive schools. *Educational Leadership, 52*(4), 64-70.

Saunders, J., & Espeland, P. (1991). *Bringing out their best: A resource guide for parents of young gifted children* (2nd ed.). Minneapolis, MN: Freespirit Publishing.

Savage, L. B. (1998). Eliciting critical thinking skills through questioning. *Clearing House, 71*(5), 291-294.

Schlichter, C. L. (1997). Talents Unlimited model in programs for gifted students. In N. Colangelo & G. A. Davis (Eds.), *Handbook of gifted education* (2nd ed.). Boston: Allyn & Bacon.

Shore, B. M., Cornell, D. G., Robinson, A., & Ward, V. S. (1991). *Recommended practices in gifted education: A critical analysis.* New York: Teachers College Press.

Slavin, R. E. (1991). Are cooperative learning and "untracking" harmful to the gifted? *Educational Leadership, 48*(6), 68-72.

Smith, H. L. *Dual-language programs: Lessons from two schools.* Retrieved June 27, 2002, from www.scottforesman.com/educators/letters/bilingual/smith.html

Smith, T. K., & Cestaro, N. G. (1998). *Student-centered physical education: Strategies for developing middle school fitness and skills.* Champaign, IL: Human Kinetics Publishers.

Spearman, C. E. (1927). *The abilities of man: Their nature and measurement.* London: McMillan.

Stanford, P., & Siders, J. (2001). Accessing the curriculum: E-pal writing! *Teaching Exceptional Children, 34*(2), 21-24.

Starko, A. J. (2000). Finding the problem finders: Problem finding and the identification and development of talent. In R. C. Jenkins & B. M. Shore (Eds.), *Talents unfolding* (pp. 233-249). Washington, DC: American Psychological Association.

Stepien, W. J. (2001). *The Internet and problem-based learning: developing solutions through the Web.* Tucson, AZ: Zephyr Press.

Sternberg, R. J. (1986). *Beyond IQ: A teacher's theory of human intelligence.* Cambridge, UK: Cambridge University Press.

Sternberg, R. J. (1990). What constitutes a "good" definition of giftedness? *Journal for the Education of the Gifted, 14,* 96-100.

Tallent-Runnels, M. K., & Candler-Lotven, A. C. (1996). *Academic competitions for gifted students: A resource book for teachers and parents.* Thousand Oaks, CA: Corwin.

Taylor, C. (1968). The multiple talent approach. *Instructor, 77*(27), 142, 144, 146.

Thomas, W. P., & Collier, V. P. (1997). Two languages are better than one. *Educational Leadership, 55*(4), 23-27.

Tomlinson, C. A., Kaplan, S. N., Renzulli, J. S., Leppien, J., & Burns, D. (2001). *The parallel curriculum.* Thousand Oaks, CA: Sage.

Torp, L., & Sage, S. (1998). *Problems as possibilities: Problem-based learning for K-12 education.* Alexandria, VA: Association for Supervision & Curriculum Development.

Treffinger, D. J. (1995). School improvement, talent development, and creativity. *Roeper Review, 18*(2), 93-98.

Treffinger, D. J. (1998). From gifted education to programming for talent development. *Phi Delta Kappan, 79*(10), 752-756.

U.S. Department of Education. (1993). *National excellence: A case for developing America's talent.* Washington, DC: Author.

Vancleave, J. (2000). *Janice Vancleave's guide to more of the best science projects.* New York: John Wiley.

VanTassel-Baska, J. (1994). *Comprehensive curriculum for gifted learners* (2nd ed.). Boston: Allyn & Bacon.

VanTassel-Baska, J. (1998). The development of academic talent: A mandate for educational best practice. *Phi Delta Kappan, 7*(10), 760-764.

VanTassel-Baska, J. (2001). The role of advanced placement in talent development. *Journal of Secondary Gifted Education, 12*(3), 126-132.

Wagner, R. K. (2000). Practical intelligence. In R. J. Sternberg (Ed.), *Handbook of intelligence* (pp. 380-395). New York: Cambridge University Press.

Westberg, K. L., Archambault, F. X., Dobyns, S. M., & Slavin, T. J. (1992). *Technical report: An observational study of instructional and curricular practices used with gifted and talented students in regular classrooms.* Storrs: University of Connecticut, National Research Center on the Gifted and Talented.

Willis, S. (1990). Cooperative learning fallout. *ASCD Update 32*(8), 6, 8.

Zemelman, S., Daniels, H., & Hyde, A. (1993). *Best practice: New standards for teaching and learning in America's schools.* Portsmouth, NH: Heinemann.

Index

**CORWIN
PRESS**

The Corwin Press logo—a raven striding across an open book—represents the happy union of courage and learning. We are a professional-level publisher of books and journals for K-12 educators, and we are committed to creating and providing resources that embody these qualities. Corwin's motto is "Success for All Learners."